Principles and Practices of Banking

Dr.S. Umamaheswari

Dr.T. Priyanka

Dr.S. Joyce

Dr.M. Soundarya

Published by

BONFRING®
Intellectual Integrity

Principles and Practices of Banking

9 788196 818814 >

ISBN 978-81-968188-1-4

Price: ₹279

Authors

Dr.S. Umamaheswari | Dr.T. Priyanka | Dr.S. Joyce | Dr.M. Soundarya

Bonfring

309, 5th Street Extension, Gandhipuram,

Coimbatore - 641 012,

Tamil Nadu, India.

E-mail: info@bonfring.org

Website: www.bonfring.org

Preface

During the last ten years banking field has developed enormously in day-to-day life and banking transactions has been done by each and every human being. This book continues along the path started by the first two in this series by discussing bank operations. It takes a new tack, however, by looking at how banks operate in a legal and regulatory light and delves deep into laws and regulations and how banks can shape their practices to meet all the necessary legal and regulatory requirements.

This book is distinguished by the unique approach that it takes while dealing the subject, the book chapters contain five units related topics such as relationship between banking and customers, Types of deposits, Cheque, Endorsement, Protection and Forgery of Customer's Signature, collecting banker and Paying Banker.

Dr.S. Umamaheswari

Dr.T. Priyanka

Dr.S. Joyce

Dr.M. Soundarya

TABLE OF CONTENTS

Unit-I

Banker and Customer – Meaning – definition – Relationship – General and Special – obligation to honor cheque – lien – obligation to maintain secrecy of customer's account – right to charge compound interest – Individual charge charges.

Unit-II

Bankers as Borrowers: Saving Deposit – Current Deposit – Fixed Deposit Receipts and its legal implications – Pass book – Meaning and Maintenance – Prober Function – Effect of entries favorable to a customer – Effect of entries favorable to a bankers. Special types of customer – General procedure for opening accounts – Minors – Firms – limited Companies – Non – trading Concerns – Joint Account.

Unit-III

Cheque – Meaning – definition – essentials – Cheque Vs. Bill of Exchange – Proper drawing of Cheques – banking of Cheques – Offence under Sec. 138 of the NI Act. Material Alteration– Case Law – Illustration – Examples – Banker's Duty – Immaterial Alteration, Marking – Meaning – Significance – Crossing – Meaning – Definition – Forms and significance of various forms of crossing.

Unit-IV

Endorsement – Meaning – definition – Kinds of Endorsement – Paying Banker – Meaning – Significance of Paying Banker – Circumstances for dishonor of cheques – Statutory protection under Sec. 85 of the NI Act – Protection and Forgery of Customer's Signature.

Unit-V

Collecting Banker – duties – Statutory protection under Sec. 131 of the NI Act – Concept of Negligence. Knowledge of various forms used in day – to – day Banking: Cheque – Pay – in Slip – Withdrawal Form – Transfer form – Draft – Bill of Exchange – Promissory Note – FDR – Safe Custody Receipt – Travelers' Cheque – Credit Card – Letter of Credit.

UNIT-I

INTRODUCTION TO BANKING

1.1. Introduction

The banking sector is the lifeline of any modern economy. It is one of the important financial pillars of the financial sector, which plays a vital role in the functioning of an economy. It is very important for economic development of a country that its financing requirements of trade, industry and agriculture are met with higher degree of commitment and responsibility. Thus, the development of a country is integrally linked with the development of banking. In modern economy banks are to be considered not as dealers in money but as the leaders of development. They play an important role in the mobilization of deposits and disbursement of credit to various sectors of the economy. The banking system reflects the economic health of the country. The strength of an economy depends on a sound and solvent banking system. A sound banking system efficiently mobilized savings in productive sector and a solvent banking system ensures that the bank is capable of meeting its obligation to the depositors.

A bank may be defined as an institution that accepts deposits, makes loans, pays checks, and provides financial services. A bank is a financial intermediary for the safeguarding, transferring, exchanging, or lending of money. A primary role of banks is connecting those with funds, such as investors and depositors, to those seeking funds, such as individuals or businesses needing loans. A bank is the connection between customers that have capital deficits and customers with capital surpluses.

A bank is a financial institution and financial intermediaries that accepts deposits and channelize them into lending activities, either directly or through capital markets. Banking in India originated in the last decades of the 18th century. The first bank was the general Bank of India, which started in 1786, and Bank of Hindustan which was started in 1970, both are now defunct. Later the Bank of Bengal in 1809, Bank of Bombay in 1840 and Bank of Madras in 1843 these three presidency banks were merged in 1921 to form the Imperial Bank of India and converted into State Bank of India in 1955. In 1969, 14 banks were nationalized and in the second phase of nationalization six more banks were nationalized in 1980. The need for nationalization was mainly the private commercial banks were not fulfilling the social and developmental goals of banking which are so essential for any industrial economy. The RBI was established in 1935, as the central bank of India regulate to the financial and banking system and it formulates monetary policy and prescribes exchange control norms. The banking regulation act 1949 and RBI act 1934 authorize the RBI to regulate the banking sector in India. There are currently 27 public sector banks in India , out of which 19 are nationalized banks and 6 are SBI and its associate banks, and rest two are IDBI Bank and Bharatiya Mahila Bank, which are categorized as other public sector banks.

1.2. Functions of Banking

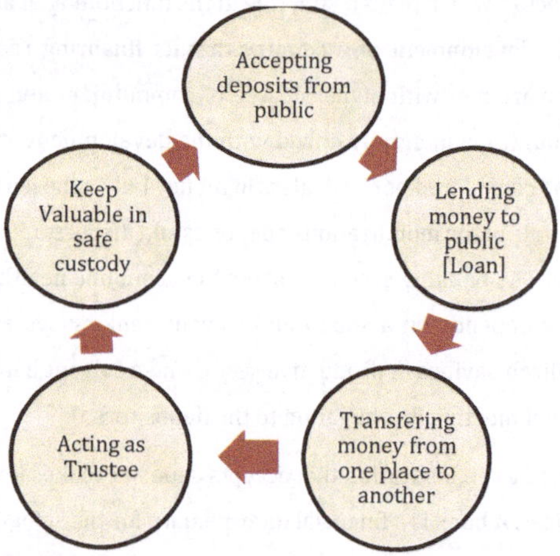

1.3. Evolution of Banking

- Pre- Independence Phase - 1947
- Second phase – 1947 -1991
- Third phase – The LPG 1991.

Pre- Independence Phase - 1947

This phase is characterized by the presence of large number of banks (more than 600). Banking system commenced in India with the foundation of Bank of Hindustan in calcutta in 1770 which ceased to operate in 1832. After that many banks came but were not successful like General Bank of India (1786-1791), Oudh commercial bank of India. Whereas some are successful and continue to lead even now like Allahabad Bank (1865), Punjab National Bank (1894), Bank of India (1906), Bank of Baroda (1908), Central Bank of India (1911) While some others like Bank of Bengal (1806), Bank of Bombay (1840), Bank of madras (1843) merged into a single entity in 1921 which came to be known as Imperial Bank of India. Imperial Bank of India was later renamed in 1955 as the SBI. In April 1935, Reserve Bank of India was formed based on the recommendation of Hilton Young Commission set up in 1926.

In this time period, most of the bank were small in size and suffered from a high rate of failures. As a result, public confidence is low in this banks and deposit mobilization was also very slow. People continued to rely on the unorganized sector (Money lenders and Indigenous Bankers).

Second Phase – (1947-1991)

Broadly the main characteristic feature of this phase is the Nationalization of the bank. With the view of economic planning, nationalization emerged as an effective measure.

Need for Nationalization in India

- The banks mostly catered to the needs of large industries, big business houses.
- Sectors such as agriculture, small-scale industries and exports were lagging behind.
- The poor masses continued to be exploited by the moneylenders.

Following this, in the year 1949, 1st January the Reserve Bank of India was nationalized. Fourteen commercial banks were nationalized on 19th July 1969. Smt. Indira Gandhi was the Prime Minister of India, during in 1969. The following banks are nationalized:

- Central Bank of India
- Bank of India
- Punjab National Bank
- Bank of Baroda
- United Commercial Bank
- Canara Bank
- Dena Bank
- United Bank
- Syndicate Bank
- Allahabad Bank
- Indian Bank
- Union Bank of India
- Bank of Maharashtra
- Indian Overseas Bank

Six more commercial banks were nationalized in April 1980. These are mentioned below:

- Andhra Bank
- Corporation Bank
- New Bank of India
- Oriental Bank of Commerce
- Punjab & Sindh Bank
- Vijaya Bank.

Meanwhile, on the recommendation of the Narasimham committee, Regional Rural Banks (RRBs) were formed on Oct 2, 1975. The objective behind the formation of RRBs was to serve the large unserved population of rural areas and promoting financial inclusion. With a view to meet the specific requirement from the different sector (i.e. agriculture, housing, foreign trade, industry) some apex level banking institutions were also set up like:

- NABARD (est. 1982)
- EXIM (est. 1982)
- NHB (est. 1988)
- SIDBI (est. 1990)

Third Phase 1991 and Beyond

- This period saw remarkable growth in the process of development of banks with the liberalization of economic policies.
- Even after nationalization and the subsequent regulations that followed, a large portion of masses is untouched by the banking services.
- Considering this, in 1991, the Narasimham committee gave its recommendation i.e. to allow the entry of private sector players into the banking system.
- Following this, RBI gave license to 10 private entities, out of which few survived the market demands, which are- ICICI, HDFC, Axis Bank, IndusInd Bank, DCB.
- In 1998, the Narsimham committee again recommended the entry of more private players. As a result, RBI gave a license to the following newbies:
  - Kotak Mahindra Bank (2001)
  - Yes Bank (2004)
- In 2013-14, the third round of bank licensing took place and in 2015, IDFC bank and Bandhan Bank emerged.

- In order to further financial inclusion, RBI also proposed to set up 2 new kinds of banks i.e. Payment Banks and Small Banks.
- In 2015, RBI gave in-principle licence to 11 entities to launch Payments Bank and granted 'in-principle' approval to the 10 applicants to set up Small Finance Banks.

1.4. Meaning of Banking

A bank is a financial institution licensed to receive deposits and make loans. Banks may also provide financial services such as wealth management, currency exchange, and safe deposit boxes. There are several different kinds of banks including retail banks, commercial or corporate banks, and investment banks. In most countries, banks are regulated by the national government or central bank.

1.5. Definition of Banking

According to Sec 5 (c) of the Banking Regulation Act 1949, a banker is a person who undertakes business of banking. Banking means accepting deposits from public, for the purpose of lending, repayable on demand or otherwise with drawable by cheque, draft, order.

According to P.A Samuelson, "Bank provides service to its clients and in turn receives perquisites in different forms".

According to R.P Kentt, "Bank is an Institution which collects idle money temporarily from the public and lends to other people as per need".

According to Indian Company Law 1936 defines Bank as, "a banking company which receives deposits through current account or any other forms and allows withdrawal through cheques or promissory notes.

According to Cairn Cross, "Bank is a Financial Intermediary Institution which deals in loans and advances".

1.6. Meaning of Customer

A Customer is a person who has some sort of account, either deposit or current account, with the banker.

1.7. Definition of Customer

According to Dr. Hart, "a customer is one who has an account with a banker or for whom banker habitually undertakes to act as such."

According to Sir John Paget's, "a customer there must be some recognizable course or habit of dealing in the nature of regular banking business".

As per Reserve Bank of India report customer can be defined as, "a customer can be defined as a user or a potential user of bank services". So defined, a 'Customer' may include:

- a person or entity that maintains an account and/or has a business relationship with the bank;
- one on whose behalf the account is maintained (i.e. the beneficial owner);
- beneficiaries of transactions conducted by professional intermediaries, such as Stock Brokers, Chartered Accountants, Solicitors, etc., as permitted under the law, and
- any person or entity connected with a financial transaction which can pose significant reputational or other risks to the bank, say, a wire transfer or issue of a high value demand draft as a single transaction.

One may conclude that a "Customer" is one who has either a current or a deposit account or, in the absence of it, some relation with the bank in the ordinary course of business, that can be seen as banking business.

1.8. Relationship between Banker and Customer

Customers are those who avail a service of any goods and services provided by the manufacturer or service provider with due consideration of money. In the same way the moment an individual opens an account with the banker, then he/ she becomes a customer of the bank. Then there exists a special relationship of different duties and obligations between customer and banker. Relation between banker and customer is consensual depending on express or implied contract between two. Thereby a contractual relation springs between banker and customer. In case of banking where a person asks the banker to open an account for him and the banker's acceptance thereof, constitutes implied contract of relationship.

Relation of banker and customer depends upon the service given by the banker. In addition to his primary functions, a banker renders a number of services to his customer. The relationship between them primarily is that of a creditor and debtor. A banker also act as an agent or trustee of his customer if the latter entrusts the former with agency or trust work. In such cases, the banker act as a debtor, an agent and a trustee simultaneously but in relation to the specified business.

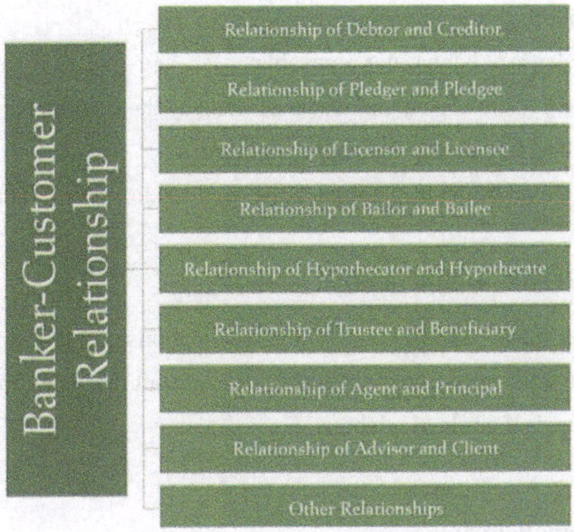

Types of Relationship

- General Relationship
- Special Relationship

General Relationship of banker and customer:

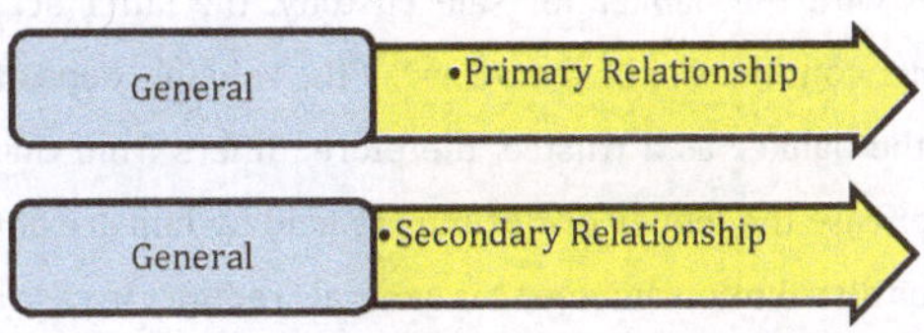

1. *Relationship as Debtor and Creditor*

The moment the customer opens an account with the banker, he/she becomes debtor of the customer and the customer becomes his creditor. The banker is then bound to return an equivalent amount of money, by paying a similar sum to the depositor when he/ she is asked for it. In the same way banker also the creditor when any of the customer take the loan and any kind of advances from the bank then the customer is the debtor and the banker is creditor. Then customer (debtor) is bound to pay the loan amount to the banker (creditor) on the prescribed period of time.

Features of Debtor and Creditor

- Banker is called a dignified debtor.

- Customer is not the secured creditor of the bank.
- Customer's balance at bank is not repayable.
- Banker should pay the deposit money on demand by the customer.
- The deposit should be paid at the appropriate place.
- The demand should be made by the customer on working days and during the business hours.

2. *Relationship as Creditor and Debtor*

The banker acts as a creditor, the debtor creditor relationship holds good in the case of deposit account. But in the case of loan cash credit and overdraft the banker becomes a creditor and the customer assumes the role of a debtor.

Special Relationship

1. *Trustees and Beneficiary*

"Banker as a trustee and Customer as a beneficiary". Ordinarily, a banker is a debtor of his customer in respect of the deposits made by the latter, but in certain circumstances he/she acts as a trustee also. A trustee holds money or assets and performs certain functions for the benefit of some other person called the beneficiary. For example, if the customer deposit securities or valuables with the banker for safe custody, the latter act as a trustee of his customers. The customer continues to be the owner of the valuable deposited with the banker. The legal position of the banker as a trustee, therefore, differs from that of a debtor of his customer. In the former case the money or documents held by him are not treated as his own and are not available for distribution amongst his general creditors in case of liquidation.

2. *Agent and Principle*

"Banker as an agent and Customer as an principle". A banker acts an agent of his customer in many ways, e.g., when he/she buys or sells securities or makes payment of various dues of his customers, or collects cheques on his behalf. In all these cases, the banker acts an agent of his customer. Sec.182 of „The Indian Contract Act, 1872" defines "an agent" as a person employed to do any act for another or to represent another in dealings with third persons. The person for whom such act is done or who is so represented is called "the Principal"

Thus, an agent is a person, who acts for and on behalf of the principal and under the latter"s express or implied authority and the acts done within such authority are binding on his principal and, the principal is liable to the party for the acts of the agent.

3. *Bailor and Bailee*

"Banker as bailee and customer as bailor". In addition to the above-mentioned relations, there lao exists the relationship of bailment between the Banker and the customer. Safe custody facility is one of the numerous facilities provided by commercial banks. In this case, the legal relationship of bailment arises between the customer and the banker, whereby customer depositing with the bank is the bailor and the bank acts as the bailee. In case, where the bank does not charge any fees for such a purpose, the bank can be termed as a gratuitous bailee. In case, where a fee is charged, the bank becomes the bailee for reward. Where bank offers safe custody facility to the customer, it takes a charge of goods, articles, securities, belonging to the customer, as a bailee and not as a trustee or an agent.

4. *Pledger and Pledgee Relationship*

"Customer is the pledger and banker is the pledgee". Pledge means the bailment of goods as security for payment of a debt or performance of a promise. When credit facility is provided by bank to its customers against collateral security of movable property, the relationship of pledger and pledgee is established.

5. *Licensor and Licensee Relationship*

"Banker as Licensor and customer as Licensee", When the banker gives a safe deposit locker to the customer, the banker will become the Licensor and the customer will become the Licensee.

6. *Hypothecator and Hypothecatee*

When the customer hypothecates (pledges) certain movable or non-movable property or assets with the banker in order to get a loan, the customer became the Hypothecator, and the Banker became the Hypothecatee.

7. *Advisor and Client*

When a customer invests in securities, the banker acts as an advisor. The advice can be given officially or unofficially. While giving advice the banker has to take maximum care and caution. Here, the banker is an Advisor, and the customer is a client.

Other Relationship

1. Lessor and Lessee

The banks provide safe deposit lockers to the customers who hire them on lease basis. The relationship therefore, is that of lessee and lessor. In certain banks, this relationship is termed as Licensee and Licensor. The bank leases out the space for the use of clients. The bank is not responsible for any loss that arises to the lessee in the form of transaction except due to negligence of that bank.

2. Indemnifier and Indemnified

The customer is Indemnifier and the bank is indemnified. A Contract by which one party promises to save the other from loss caused to him by the conduct of the promisor himself or the conduct of any other person is called a contract of Indemnity - Sec 124 (Indian Contract Act,1872). In the case of banking, this relationship happens in transactions of issue of duplicate demand draft, fixed deposit, receipt etc. The underlying point in these cases is that either party will compensate the other of any loss arising from the wrong/ excess payment.

1.9. Cheque

"**Cheque** is an instrument in writing containing an unconditional order, addressed to a banker, sign by the person who has deposited money with the banker, requiring him to pay on demand a certain sum of money only to or to the order of certain person or to the bearer of instrument."

Cheque is an important instrument which can be transferred by mere and delivery. Cheque is used to make safe and convenient payment. It is less risky and the danger of loss is minimized. All cheques are bill of exchange but all the bills of exchange are not Cheque.

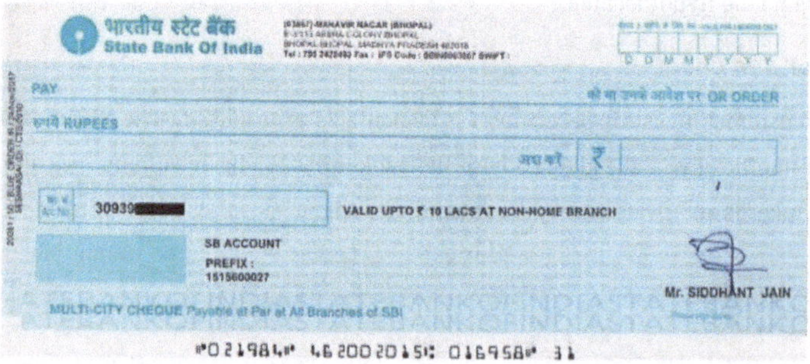

Obligation to Honor Cheque

The deposited accepted by a banker are his liabilities repayable on demand or otherwise. The banker is, therefore under a statutory obligation to honor his customer's cheques in the usual course. Sec 31 of the Negotiable Instrument Act 1881, lays down that "the drawee of cheque having sufficient funds of the drawer in his hands, properly applicable to the payment must compensate the drawer for any loss or damage caused by such default".

There are a few conditions when the banker is entitled to enforce his duty to honor the cheques issued by the account holder. When the cheque has been properly drawn and is in order in all respects including the date, amount in words and clearly expressed figures. In order words, the cheque issued is neither stale, post dated nor mutilated. Also, the signature of accountholder must to tallies with the specimen recorded with the bank. Other criteria that are needed to be fulfilled before a banker can be summarized as follows:

- Sufficient balance in the customer account and the balance is applicable for payment using cheque.
- The cheque issued is presented for payment on working days and during the business hours of the particular branch of the bank where the customer registered with.
- Endorsements on the cheque issued are correct, proper and regular.
- Payment of the cheque is not countermanded by the drawer.

Cheque to be presented with reasonable Time: Generally, a cheque presented more than six months after the date of its issue is considered as a stale one. A banker is not bound to honor an updated cheque. The obligation of a banker to honor a customer's cheque is extinguished on receipt of an order from the court. This is known as Garnishee order. **Example:** Mr.X borrows money from Mr.Y Fails to repay. Mr.Y Files suit against X, under the civil procedure code and the court issues a decree and attaches the funds in Mr.X's bank account with bank account A. The order issued by the court on bank A is Known as garnishee order. Mr.Y is the Judgement creditor and Mr.X is the Judgement debtor. Bank A is Judgement debtor's debtor.

Steps Involved While Serving Garnishee Order to the Banker

- The court will issue and order called "Order nisi" directing the banker to stop payments from the customer's account explaining why the funds in the account should not be made to the banker's account.

- After hearing the banker in response to the order nisi, the court would issue an "order absolute" directing the bank to pay the entire or part of the balance of the customer account to the Judgment creditor or the court.

Garnishee Order is Not Applicable When

- The account is overdrawn
- The account is n the Joint names of the Joint debtor and other persons whereas the in the single names of the customer.
- The debt is not due to actually the customer.
- The bank is entitled to set-off the balance against the debt due to it from the Judgment debtor.
- The banker is aware that the money in the account is held by customer in the position of a trustee.
- The name of the description of the customer in the garnishee order is wrong or inaccurate.
- The account is a joint account and the order is made in the single name of the customer.
- The balance in the account at the time of receipt of the order is due to the crediting of cheques on collection.

Obligation to Maintain Secrecy of Customer's Account

It is one of the principal duties of the banker to maintain complete secrecy of the status of customer's account and failure to do so will make the bank to compensate the customer for any damage or loss suffered. However, a bank is justified in making disclosure, under the due process of law or under express or implied consent of the customer. Disclosure in the bank's interest is permitted. So also, it is an accepted custom among the bankers to disclose certain information to a fellow banker on written request. While disclosing information to others, only bare facts should be revealed and not any comments and conclusions on the matter. The disclosing bank should indicate to the other bank that in turn it should maintain secrecy.

Thus, the general rule about the secrecy of customer's accounts may be dispensed with in the following circumstances:

- Disclosure of Information required by Law
- Disclosure permitted by the Banker's Practices and Usages

Disclosure of Information Required by Law

A banker is under statutory obligation to disclose the information relating to his customer's account when the law specially requires him to do so. The banker would, therefore, be justified in disclosing information to meet statutory requirements:

- Under the Income- Tax Act, 1961
- Under the Companies Act, 1956.
- By order of the Court under the Banker's Books Evidence Act, 1891.
- Under the Reserve Bank of IndiaAct,1934
- Under the Banking Regulation Act, 1949
- Under the Gift Tax Act, 1958. Section 36 of the Gifts Tax Act, 1958
- Disclosure to Police. Under Section 94 (3) of the Criminal Procedure Code,
- Under the Foreign Exchange Management Act, 1999
- Under the Industrial Development Bank of India Act, 1964

Disclosure Permitted by the Banker's Practices and Usages

With Express or Implied Consent of the Customer: The banker will be justified in disclosing any information relating to his customer's account with the latter's consent. In fact, **the implied term** of the contract between the banker and his customer is that the former enters into a qualified obligation with the latter to abstain from disclosing information as to his affairs without his consent the consent of the customer may be expressed or implied. Express consent exists in case the customer directs the banker in writing to intimate the balance in his account or any other information to his agent, employee or consultant.

The banker would be justified in furnishing to such person only the required information and no more. It is to be noted that the banker must be very careful in disclosing the required information to the customer or his authorized representative. For example, if an oral enquiry is made at the counter, the bank employee should not speak in louder voice so as to be heard by other customers. Similarly, the pass-book must be sent to the customer through the messenger in a closed cover. A banker generally does not disclose such information to the customer over the telephone unless he can recognize the voice of his customer; otherwise, he bears the risk inherent in such disclosure.

In certain circumstances, the implied consent of the customer permits the banker to disclose necessary information. For example, if the banker sanctions a loan to a customer on the guarantee of a third person and the latter asks the banker certain questions relating to the customer's account. The banker is authorized to do so because by furnishing the name of the guarantor, the customer is presumed to have given his implied consent for such disclosure. The banker should give the relevant information correctly and in good faith.

Similarly, if the customer furnishes the name of the banker to a third party for the purpose of a trade reference, not only an express consent of the customer exists for the discloser of relevant information but the banker is directed to do so, the non – compliance of which will adversely affect the reputation of the customer. Implied consent should not be taken for granted in all cases even where the customer and the enquirer happen to be very closely related. For example, the banker should not disclose the state of a lady's account to her husband without the express consent of the customer.

The banker may disclose the state of his customer's account in order to legally protect his own interest. For example, if the banker has to recover the dues from the customer or the guarantor, disclosure of necessary facts to the guarantor or the solicitor becomes necessary and is quite justified.

Banker's Reference: Banker follows the practice of making necessary enquires about the customers, their sureties or the acceptors of the bills from other bankers. This is an established practice amongst the bankers and is justified on the ground that an implied consent of the customer is presumed to exist. By custom and practice necessary information or opinion about the customer is furnished by the banker confidentially. However, the banker should be very careful in replying to such enquiries.

1.10. Bankers Lien

Banker's lien is an enforceable right of a bank to hold in its possession any money or property belonging to a customer and to apply it to the repayment of any outstanding debt owed to the bank, provided that, to the bank's knowledge, such property is not part of a trust fund or is not already burdened with other debts. Banker's lien is both a possessory lien and a special lien.

The bank has the right to seize and sell the defaulting borrower's property in its possession, after giving a reasonable notice but without going through the foreclosure procedure. Enforcement of a banker's lien, however, may depend on the type of the property and the reason it was handed over to the bank. Bills of exchange, credit-cash balance, negotiable securities and promissory notes may be claimed under this lien. However, the borrower's property handed over to the bank for a specific purpose, such as for safe custody for sale through a department of the bank cannot be claimed under banker's lien.

Example

"Lien is a bank holding the title to a car until the car loan has been completely paid".

Types of Lien

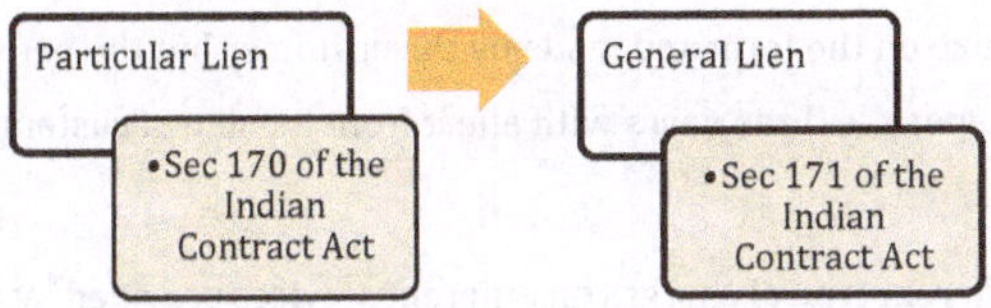

Particular Lien

Particular lien is a lien which can be exercised only on goods in respect of-which some payment is due. According to Section 170, where the bailee, in accordance with the purpose of the bailment has rendered any service which involves the exercises of the labor or skill in respect of the goods bailed, and where there is no contract to the contrary, has a right to retain such goods till the time he is paid the due remuneration for the services rendered by him. Also, the fact that, a bailee is entitled to detain only that particular property in respect of charges is due.

For Example

- A gives cloth to B, a tailor, to make into a coat. B promises A to deliver the coat as soon as it is finished, and to give a three months credit for the price. B is not entitled to retain the coat.
- A delivers a rough diamond to B, a jeweler, to be cut and polished, which is accordingly done. B is entitled to retain the stone till he is paid for the services he has rendered.

General Lien

According to Section 171 of the Indian Contract Act, general lien on the other hand, means the right to hold the goods bailed as security for a general balance of account. The right of general lien entitles the bailee to detain any goods bailed by him for any amount due to him whether in respect of those goods or some other goods. It is treated as a privilege and is specially conferred on certain kinds of bailee's only under Section 171, like the bankers, factors, wharfingers, attorneys of a high court, and policy brokers.

Right to Charge Interest

The banker has an implied right to charge interest on advances granted to its customer. Bankers generally charge interest monthly, quarterly or annually. There may be agreement between the banker and customer in this case the manner agreed will decide how interest is to be charged. As a creditor, a banker has the implied right to charge interest on the loans granted to the customer. In the same way, incidental charges like service charges, processing fees, appraisal charges, panel charges may be imposed by the banker to the customer.

Deposit is repayable on the term and made by the customer but the period of limitation for the refund of bank deposit is three years with effect from the date a customer made a demand for his money.

Bank recovers different type of charges on different services provided by them to customers.

- Bank charges interest on amount advanced,
- Processing charges for the advance,
- Bank charges for non-utilization of credit facilities sanctioned,
- Bank charges for commission, exchange, incidental charges etc. as per the terms and conditions of advance.
- Banks charge interest, at monthly, quarterly, half yearly or annually.

UNIT - II

DEPOSITS

2.1. Meaning (Deposits)

Bank deposits consist of money placed into banking institutions for safekeeping. These deposits are made to deposit accounts such as savings accounts, checking accounts and money market accounts. The account holder has the right to withdraw deposited funds, as set forth in the terms and conditions governing the account agreement. In another terms *"**A deposit account is a bank account maintained by a financial institution in which a customer can deposit money and which can be withdrawn. Deposit accounts can be savings accounts, current accounts or many other typed of bank account**".*

2.2. Types of Deposits

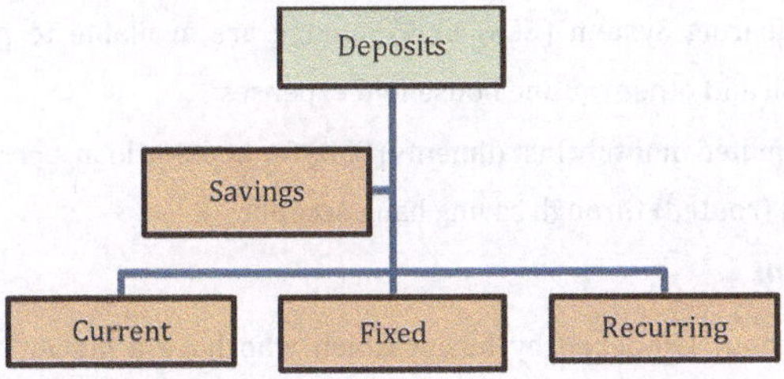

1. *Savings Account*

A savings bank account is the most basic banking facility offered by banks. A savings account is used to keep surplus funds or deposit money that will not be used immediately. Savings account has a limit on the number of monthly transactions and earn a moderate interest rate on the balance maintained. The savings account is generally opened in bank by salaried persons or by the persons who have a fixed regular income. This facility is also given to students, senior citizens, pensioners and so on.

The saving account holder is allowed to withdraw money from the account as and when required. The interest which is given on saving accounts is sometime attractive, but often nominal. At present, the rate of interest ranges between 4% to 6% per annum in India. The interest rates vary as per the amount of money deposited (lying) in the saving bank account, scheme opted, and its maturity range. It is also subject to current trend of banking policies in a country.

Features

- The main objective of saving account is to promote savings.
- There is no restriction on the number and amount of deposits. However, in India, mandatory PAN **(Permanent Account Number)** details are required to be furnished for doing cash transactions exceeding ₹50,000.
- Withdrawals are allowed subject to certain restrictions.
- The money can be withdrawn either by cheque or withdrawal slip of the respective bank.
- The rate of interest payable is very nominal on saving accounts. At present it is between 4% to 6% p.a in India.
- Saving account is of continuing nature. There is no maximum period of holding.
- A minimum amount has to be kept on saving account to keep it functioning.
- No loan facility is provided against saving account.
- Electronic clearing System (ECS) or E-Banking are available to pay electricity bill, telephone bill and other routine household expenses.
- Generally, equated monthly installments (EMI) for housing loan, personal loan, car loan, etc., are paid (routed) through saving bank account.

2. *Current Account*

Current bank account is opened by businessmen who have a higher number of regular transactions with the bank. It includes deposits, withdrawals, and contra transactions. It is also known as Demand Deposit Account. Current account can be opened in co-operative bank and commercial bank. In current account, amount can be deposited and withdrawn at any time without giving any notice. It is also suitable for making payments to creditors by using cheques. Cheques received from customers can be deposited in this account for collection.

Features

The main features of current account are as follows:

- Current bank accounts are operated to run a business.
- It is a non-interest bearing bank account.
- It needs a higher minimum balance to be maintained as compared to the savings account.
- Penalty is charged if minimum balance is not maintained in the current account.
- It charges interest on the short-term funds borrowed from the bank.

- It is of a continuing nature as there is no fixed period to hold a current account.
- It does not promote saving habits with its account holders.
- Banker requires KYC (Know your Customers) norms to be completed before opening a current account.
- The main objective of current bank account is to enable the businessmen to conduct their business transactions smoothly.
- There is no restriction on the number and amount of deposits.
- There is also no restriction on the number and amount of withdrawals made, as long as the current account holder has funds in his bank account.
- Generally, bank does not pay any interest on current account. Nowadays, some banks do pay interest on current accounts.

3. *Recurring Deposit Account*

A recurring deposit is a type of deposit in which there are fixed installments that have to be invested in an account at fixed intervals of time for a pre-decided period. Since the installments recur or fall due at regular intervals, it is called a recurring deposit. That is the recurring deposit meaning.

Different banks may specify different installment frequencies i.e monthly, quarterly, or half yearly. The most popular option offered by most banks is the monthly installment system. In this, the depositor has to pay a pre-decided amount into the recurring deposit account every month. The investor can decide the installment amount subject to the minimum rules set by the bank. It is even possible to open a recurring deposit account with an installment as low as Rs. 100.

2.3. Benefits

- A simple investment product
- Assured returns
- Flexibility of tenure and amount to be deposited
- Flexibility in withdrawal
- Loan facility
- Fixed interest rate
- Online transaction facilities

A Simple Investment Product

RD is probably the simplest financial products in the world to invest in. Even an amateur who does not have any knowledge about investment can start investing in it. As a matter of fact, many financial advisors suggest amateur investor invest in RD to develop the habit of regular savings and investment.

Assured Returns

Unlike other popular investment schemes like the mutual funds and the equity funds, recurring deposits offer assured returns on the principal amount in the short-term. Flexibility of tenure and amount to be deposited

Flexibility in Withdrawal

Recurring deposits also offer the flexibility to partially withdraw the customers' investment at any time they need. However, the customer must know that if you opt to withdraw before the end of the tenure, you would have to pay a small fee for early withdrawal. It is still a good option for customer since they can liquidate the fund in the event of an emergency.

Loan Facility

Most financial companies in India that offer recurring deposit scheme allow the investors to avail loan against their RD investment. Customers can avail loan up to 90-95% of the amount deposited in their RD account. However, different financial organizations have different policies for loan against RD deposit.

Fixed Interest Rate

The recurring deposit interest rates are fixed at the time of opening the account, and it remains the same throughout the tenure. Thus, they know the exact amount they will receive on the maturity of the deposit.

Online Transaction Facilities

Today, almost all the finance companies that offer recurring deposit facility allows the investor to access their account and do transactions online. Be it checking the balance in customers account, the maturity of the account, depositing the monthly installment or update customers residential address, customers can do it all online from the comfort from their home and at any time as per their convenience.

Fixed Deposit Account

Fixed deposit is investment instruments offered by banks and non-banking financial companies, where you can deposit money for a higher rate of interest than savings accounts. customers can deposit a lump sum of money in fixed deposit for a specific period, which varies for every financier. Once the money is invested with a reliable financier, it starts earning an interest based on the duration of the deposit. Usually, the defining criteria for FD is that the money cannot be withdrawn before maturity, but you may withdraw them after paying a penalty.

2.4. Features of Fixed Deposit

- Fixed deposits enable investors to earn higher interest on their surplus funds.
- Customers can deposit money in a fixed deposit account only once, but to deposit more money, they need to create another account.
- Though liquidity in fixed deposit is lesser, customers can look for higher rates of interests, which are higher in case of company fixed deposit
- Fixed deposit can be easily renewed
- Tax is deducted at source, from interest on Fixed Deposit as applicable, as per the Income Tax Act, 1961.

2.5. Pass Book

Passbook or Bank Statement is a copy of the account of the customer as it appears in the bank's books. When a customer deposits money and cheques into his bank account or withdraws money, he records these transactions in the bank column of his cashbook immediately. ***A passbook is maintained in the form of a ledger account with debit entries on the left-hand side and credit entries on the right-hand side. All the amounts deposited by a customer are credited and the cheques paid by banks against his accounts are credited.***

The Reserve Bank of India has made it mandatory to provide a pass book to all the saving account holders throughout the country without any additional charges.

Definition

According to Sir Jhon Paget "The proper function of pass book is to constitute a conclusive and unquestionable record of transactions between the banker and customer and it should be recognized as such"

A Pass book is a very important to a customer because it enables him to know some of the entries made by banker in his ledger account. Eg: the amount of interest allowed or charged, the incidental or other charges made by the banker. According to this view point, negligence or Omission on the part of the customer to examine the correctness of the entries in the passbook is a fault on his part and thus renders pass book record as evidence of settled and accepted account.

Specimen of Bank Passbook

Date	Particulars	Cheque No	Withdrawals	Deposits	Balance	Initaials
10.05.2020	677589932 Deposited By self	23495	Clr Mod. Balance	Dr.Rs.250	Cr.RS.250	

Features

A pass book resembles a lot like a ledger and all the transactions are entered by the banker. It too has a debit column and credit column to enter the deposits and withdrawals. A brief description of each transaction will be given in the descriptive column. This enables the account holder to have a clear idea of his transactions. Its main function is to act as a unquestionable record of banking transactions between the customer and the banker. If customer notice any change in the entries made in their pass book, they will have to bring it to the attention of the concerned person then and there. It is considered to be the duty of the account holder to examine his pass book for any wrong entries. The bank will also not acknowledge the deposit of any sum that is not mentioned in their pass book. Hence examine customers pass book and get the transactions recorded once in a while.

2.6. Advantages of Pass Book

- Safer Transactions
- Easy to focus on savings

Safer Transactions

Some people feel that passbook savings accounts offer safer transactions. Not everyone trusts ATM machines--a number of people feel the machines are confusing and unsafe. These customers want to actually see who is handling their money. A passbook savings account allows for face-to-face contact that puts some people at ease.

Easy to Focus on Saving

With a passbook savings account, customers do not use an ATM card to withdraw their funds withdrawals must be made in person. This helps customers to save their money because it is less likely that customers will make a frivolous purchase. If customers want to make a withdrawal, they have to go to the bank, fill out a slip, and hand it to the teller. The transaction is entered in the passbook. This gives customers more time to think about the transaction than if customers simply swipe a card.

2.7. Disadvantages of Pass book

Low Barrier to Entry

Passbook savings accounts are great for those who want to save without worrying about minimum balances and monthly fees. These accounts usually have no fees or monthly balance requirements; in exchange, they offer lower interest rates, a potential disadvantage.

Low Interest Rates

The main disadvantage to passbook savings account is their low interest rates. If customers are looking to make a high return on their money, a passbook savings account is not a good option. According to Bankrate.com, the average national APY was less than 1 percent as of December 2010. However, if customers just want to have liquid funds available in case of any emergency, this may not be of concern to customers.

No Monthly Statement

With a passbook savings account, customers do not receive a monthly statement. Customers have to make sure the deposits, withdrawals, and interest are recorded in customers' booklet. If customers are not very organized, this can be a big disadvantage.

Effect of Entries Favorable to a Customer in Pass Book

The account of a customer may sometimes wrongly show a credit balance, which is larger than the correct balance because of duplication of credit entries or incorrectly entering higher amounts for such entries or due to omission of any debit entry. The legal position of the banker and his customer shall be as follows:

The pass book is written by the banker and hence the entries therein may form evidence against the banker. The customer is rightly entitled to believe them as correct and to act on the basis of such entries. If the Pass Book shows a higher balance and the customer withdraws such balance treating it as his own and subsequently spends it away, the banker shall not be entitled to recover such amount wrongly paid to the customer. But the customer shall have to prove that

- He acted in such manner relying on the correctness of the balance shown in the Pass Book and had no knowledge of the mistakes therein, and
- He altered his position by spending the same. This benefit has been given to the customer in various judgments because of the presumption that normally a person spends what customers presumes to belong to him and if the banker permits him to withdraw excess money on the above presumption, it would be a great prejudice to him, if customers is called to pay them back.

Effect of Entries Favorable to a Bankers

When a credit entry has been totally omitted or its figure has been wrongly stated or any debit entry has been erroneously made in the account of the customer, such entries are favorable to the banker and against the customer. The customer is entitled to get the mistake rectified as soon as he happens to detect it. This right of the customer does not lapse even if he returns the Pass Book without raising objection regarding any entry or he remains silent after the receipt of the Pass Book because, as already noted, the customer is not bound to examine the Pass Book periodically and regularly. He is entitled to recover the amount wrongly debited to, or omitted to be credited to his account. The right of the customer to get the mistake rectified is, however, subject to one limitation. If the customer comes to know about the forgery in the cheque and he does not inform the bank, it will constitute a negligence on his part. The customer will, therefore, not be entitled to recover the amount paid by the banker on the forged cheque.

Precautions taken by the Banker & Customer

- The Pass Book must be sent by the customer to the bank periodically and regularly for recording the necessary entries, so that mistakes, if any, may be detected by the customer soon thereafter. Reserve Bank has advised the banks to issue a simple receipt to the tenderer of savings bank Pass Book if it is retained by the Bank for updating.
- The Pass Book must be initialed by the accountant or other responsible officer of the Bank, who must ascertain the accuracy of the balance on the date of recording the entries; otherwise, the customer will be entitled to act upon the same, if it is wrongly stated.

- The customer must tally the entries with his own record—either the account books or customer counterfoils of pay-in-slips and cheques, etc. If any accuracy is found, the customer must inform the bank immediately to get the mistake rectified.
- While sending the Pass Book to the customer, the banker should take steps to ensure the secrecy of its contents. The Pass Book must be sent in a closed cover.

2.8. Customer

A person who has a bank account in his name and for whom the banker undertakes to provide the facilities as a banker is considered to be a customer.

To constitute a customer the following requirements must be fulfilled;

- The bank account may be savings, current or fixed deposit must be operated in his name by making a necessary deposit of money.
- The dealing between the banker and customer must be of the nature of the banking business.

Definition

A customer is a person who is utilizing one or more of the services provided by the bank. A customer is a person through whom the bank gets an opportunity to make an earning in return to the service they can provide the customer with. ***For Ex:*** *An individual who has a checking account with a bank or an individual who has a mortgage or a loan with the bank or an individual who has a fixed deposit with the bank are all customers of the bank.*

2.9. Special Types of Customer

- Minors
- Individuals
- Lunatics
- Illiterate persons
- Married women
- Executors and administrators
- Trustees
- Drunkard
- Joint accounts
- Partnership firm

Minors

A minor is a person who has not completed 18 years of age. In case a guardian of his person or property is appointed by a court of law before he completes his 18 years, the period of minority is extended to the completion of 21 years. As per section 11 of the contract act a minor is incompetent to contract but section 26 of the Negotiable Instrument Act allows a minor to draw, endorse, deliver and negotiate a negotiable instrument.

Lunatics

A person of unsound mind cannot make a valid contract. So, the bankers should not open an account in the name of a person of unsound mind. But a customer may become lunatic after opening an account with the bank.

Illiterate Persons

An illiterate person means a person who can't sign his name. While opening of an account of such a person is unavoidable, the banker should obtain

- Left thumb impression on the account opening form and specimen signature card in the presence of an authorized bank official
- Details of identification marks should be noted on the account opening form and specimen signature card
- At least two copies of photograph duly attested by any account holder/authorized bank official.

Married Women

A Married woman can enter into contract and bind her personal (separate) estate. A banker may, therefore, open an account in the name of a married woman.

Executors & Administrators

Executors and Administrators are allowed to open bank account. Formalities are to be observed while opening the account in the name of executor/administrator.

Trustees

A banker must be cautions in opening/operating a trust account as the trustees are responsible for public money. Trusts are created by the settler by executing a Trust Deed. A trust account can be opened only after obtaining and scrutinizing the trust deed. The Trust account has to be operated by all the trustees jointly unless provided otherwise in the trust deed. A trustee cannot delegate the powers to other Trustees except as provided for in the Trust Deed. A cheque favoring the Trust shall not be credited to the personal account of the Trustee.

Drunkard

A drunkard is a person who is so toxicities to be incapable of understanding the nature and effect of a contract upon his interest. A contract entered to a drunkard person is void. It is advisable for banker to not allow a drunkard to start an account in his name.

Joint Accounts

A joint stock company is an artificial person and it has a separate legal entity. So, a bank account may be opened on its own name. A joint stock company may either be a Private Limited Company or a Public Limited Company.

Partnership Firm

A firms account should always be opened in the name of the firm and not in the name(s) of the individual partner (s) because a partner does not have (implied) authority to open a bank account on behalf of the firm in his own name. A is not a legal entity independent of partners. It is an association of persons. Registration of a partnership is not compulsory under Partnership Act. However, many banks insist on registration of a partnership. In any case, ie stamped partnership deed or Partnership letter should be taken when an account is opened for a partnership. The partnership deed will contain names of the partners, objective of the partnership, and other operational details, which should be taken note of by the bank in its dealings.

Procedure for Opening a Bank Account

Public starts their bank relationship mostly opening a Savings bank account (SB Account) depositing small sums of amounts as and when they have surplus money in their hand. To open a deposit account, person has to fill up an account opening application form, submit to the concerned branch. ***Application form should be accompanied with the following documents in order to avoid misuse or illegal dealings:***

- Introductory reference of an acceptable person or an existing account holder with the branch.
- Acceptable proof of his / her identity and residential address. It may be one of Aadhaar Card / photo identity card such as Passport, Ration card, PAN card, Driving license, Election identity card etc.

- Recent photographs (2 to 3 varies from bank to bank, branch to branch).
- An initial deposit amount not less than the minimum amount decided by the bank (amount varies from bank-to-bank ranging from 0 to Rs 10,000/ or even more).
- The bank keeps attested photo copies of all the documents along with the account opening form.

Know your Customer (KYC) Guidelines of RBI

In 2002, RBI issued an order to all banks to follow the procedure of **"Know Your Customer"** with all their new and existing Domestic customers and Non-resident customers. It helps to verify the identity and residential address of the customers with the help of specific documental evidence. Hence, proper KYC prevents misuse of the banking system for money laundering and financing of terrorist activities. The "Rules" would help to stop illegal moneys coming into the banking stream. It is mandatory requirement to all religious and non-religious trust accounts should also have to follow all KYC processes. The RBI needs all banks to strictly follow the KYC guidelines and cash transaction norms. The KYC Rules of RBI support the existing practice of some banks and makes it a compulsory requirement to be followed by all the banks in regard to all of their customers who maintain domestic / Non-resident rupee / foreign currency accounts.

2.10. Minor's Account

A minor is a person who has not completed 18 years of age. In case a guardian of his person or property is appointed by a court of law before he completes his 18 years, the period of minority is extended to the completion of 21 years. As per section 11 of the contract act a minor is incompetent to contract but section 26 of the Negotiable Instrument Act allows a minor to draw, endorse, deliver and negotiate a negotiable instrument. Children's bank accounts help parents create a corpus for their children and teach them basics of money management. Such accounts are called "Minor" accounts.

Who can open the Account?

- A natural guardian on behalf of the minor.
- A natural guardian, jointly with the minor.
- A legal guardian in the name of the minor.
- A minor of age 10 and above in his/her name to be operated by the minor.
- The usual account opening form can be filled up to open a minor account. Details like the minor's name, address, guardian details and signature must be furnished.

General Procedure for Opening a Bank Account

- Proof of minor's date of birth
- KYC documents of the guardian.
- Aadhaar card of the minor.
- Specimen signature of guardian.
- Minor's specimen signature in case he/she is 10 years old.

Operation of Account

For accounts of minors below 10 years of age, the guardian must operate the account. However, minors over 10 years of age can operate the account on their own.

Upon Turning 18 Years

Once the minor turns 18, the account has to be designated as a regular savings account. Thereafter, the guardian cannot operate the account on the account holder's behalf. An application form along with KYC of minor turned major needs to be furnished

2.11. Firms: (Meaning)

A firm is a commercial enterprise, a company that buys and sells products and/or services to consumers with the aim of making a profit. A business entity such as a corporation, limited liability company, public limited company, sole proprietorship, or partnership that has products or services for sale is a firm.

Definition

Some definitions of firm given by renowned economists are given below.

- Firm is a unit of production that employs factors of production (or inputs) to produce goods & services under given state of technology.
- It is an independently administered business unit – **Hanson.**
- It is a center of control where the decisions about what to produce & how to produce are taken.
- It is a business unit which hires productive resources for the purpose of producing goods & services.
- A firm is an independent organization whose destiny is determined by the magnitude of the aggregate pay off & in which the aggregate pay off production & sale of goods or services **(Harvey Leibenstein).**

Types of Firms

- Private Ltd Company
- Public Ltd Company
- Unlimited Company
- Sole proprietorship
- Joint Hindu Family business
- Partnership
- Cooperatives
- Limited Liability Partnership (LLP)

1. Private Limited Company

A private limited company is a company which is privately held for small businesses. The liability of the members of a Private Limited Company is limited to the amount of shares respectively held by them. Shares of Private Limited Company cannot be publically traded.

Characteristics of Private Limited Company

- **Members**– To start a company, a minimum number of 2 members are required and a maximum number of 200 members as per the provisions of the **Companies Act, 2013**.
- **Limited Liability**– The liability of each member or shareholders is limited. It means that if a company faces loss under any circumstances, then its shareholders are liable to sell their own assets for payment. The personal, individual assets of the shareholders are not at risk.
- **Perpetual succession**– The company keeps on existing in the eyes of law even in the case of death, insolvency, the bankruptcy of any of its members. This leads to the perpetual succession of the company. The life of the company keeps on existing forever.
- **Index of members**– A private company has a privilege over the public company as they don't have to keep an index of its members whereas the public company is required to maintain an index of its members.
- **A number of directors**– When it comes to directors a private company needs to have only two directors. With the existence of 2 directors, a private company can come into operations.
- **Paid-up capital**– It must have a minimum paid-up capital of Rs 1 lakh or such higher amount which may be prescribed from time to time.

- **Prospectus**– Prospectus is a detailed statement of the company affairs that is issued by a company for its public. However, in the case of **a private limited company**, there is no such need to issue a prospectus because this public is not invited to subscribe for the shares of the company.
- **Minimum subscription**– It is the amount received by the company which is 90% of the shares issued within a certain period of time. If the company is not able to receive 90% of the amount then they cannot commence further business. In the case of a private limited company, shares can be allotted to the public without receiving the minimum subscription.
- **Name**– It is mandatory for all the private companies to use the word private limited after its name.

2. *Public Limited Company*

A Public Limited Company (PLC) is a separate legal business entity which offers its shares to be traded on the stock exchange for the general public. According to the regulations of the corporate law, a PLC has to compulsorily present its financial stats and position publicly to maintain transparency.

Characteristics of Public Limited Company

- **Ownership**: The ownership of a PLC lies with two or more shareholders who own the shares of the company.
- **Index of Members**: A public limited company needs to keep an index of its members with their names.
- **Paid Up Capital**: The company needs to have a minimum paid-up capital as decided by the corporate law of that country. According to the Companies Act, 2013, a PLC in India needs to keep rupees five lacs as a minimum paid-up capital.
- **Perpetual Succession**: The company's existence is independent of the death, bankruptcy or insolvency of any of the member.
- **Formation**: A PLC can be formed with the appointment of at least two directors and one qualified company secretary.
- **Directors**: A public company needs to have three or more directors for its existence.
- **Name**: The company has to end its registered name with the word 'limited' for making it a PLC.

- **Limited Liability**: The liability of the shareholders of a public limited company in case of loss or debts is only limited to the amount of investment they have made in the company. Their assets cannot be charged liable for any such damages.
- **Prospectus**: It is mandatory for a public limited company to issue a prospectus which is the statement of present and plans of the company.
- **Abided by Law**: A public limited company has to abide by the corporate laws of the country. Indian PLCs have to follow the regulations of the Companies Act, 2013.
- **Minimum Subscription**: A PLC needs to acquire at least 90% amount of the shares issued by the company within a particular period.

3. *Unlimited Company*

An unlimited company is a type of private company. It has some features similar to a limited company. However, the shareholders (or members) of this type of company have unlimited liability. This means each member is jointly and severally liable for the debts of the company in the event of its insolvent winding-up.

Advantages of the Unlimited Liability Company

- Registration of the Unlimited Liability Company can be made without share capital.
- Unlimited Liability Company can use, reduce or increase its share capital without any restrictions.
- To modify the share capital a special resolution with an application need to submit.
- A statutory meeting is not required in case of Unlimited Company.
- In Unlimited Liability Company someone can purchase its own share.
- Any person can purchase its own share, The section 67 is not applied to Unlimited Liability Company.

4. *Sole Proprietorship*

A sole proprietorship, also known as the sole trader or simply a proprietorship, is a type of business entity that is owned and run by one natural person and in which there is no legal distinction between the owner and the business. The owner is in direct control of all elements and is legally accountable for the finances of such business and this may include debts, loans, loss etc.

The Advantages of a Sole Proprietorship Include

- Owners can establish a sole proprietorship instantly, easily and inexpensively.

- Sole proprietorships carry little, if any, ongoing formalities.
- A sole proprietor need not pay unemployment tax on himself or herself (although he or she must pay unemployment tax on employees).
- Owners may freely mix business or personal assets.

The Disadvantages of a Sole Proprietorship Include

- Owners are subject to unlimited personal liability for the debts, losses and liabilities of the business.
- Owners cannot raise capital by selling an interest in the business.
- Sole proprietorships rarely survive the death or incapacity of their owners and so do not retain value.

5. *Joint Hindu Family Business*

The Joint Hindu Family Business is a distinct form of organization peculiar to India. Joint Hindu Family Firm is created by the operation of law. It does not have any separate and distinct legal entity from that of its members. The business of Joint Hindu Family is controlled under the Hindu Law instead of Partnership Act. The membership in this form of business organization can be acquired only by birth or by marriage to a male person who is already a member of Joint Hindu Family.

"When two or more families agree to live and work together, throw their resources and labour with joint stock and share profits and the losses together, then this family is known as composite family."

Characteristics of a Joint Hindu Family Business

Governed by Hindu Law

The business of the Joint Hindu Family is controlled and managed under the Hindu law.

There are two schools of Hindu law

- Dayabhaga, and
- Mitakshara.

Management

All the affairs of a Joint Hindu Family are controlled and managed by one person who is known as 'Karta' or 'Manager'. The Karta is the senior most male member of the family. He works in consultation with other members of the family but ultimately, he has a final say.

The members of the family have full faith and confidence in Karta. Only Karta is entitled to deal with outsiders. But other members can deal with outsiders only with the permission of Karta.

Membership by Birth

The membership of the family can be acquired only by birth. As soon as a male child is born in family, he becomes a member. Membership requires no consent or agreement.

Liability

Except the Karta, the liability of all other members is limited to their shares in the business. The Karta is not only liable to the extent of his share in the business but his separate property is equally attachable and amount of debt can be recovered from his separate property.

Permanent Existence

The death, lunacy or insolvency of any member of the family does not affect the existence of the business of Joint Hindu Family. The family goes on doing its business.

Implied Authority of Karta

In a joint family firm, only Karta has the implied authority to contract debts and pledge the credit and property of the firm for the ordinary purpose of the businesses of the firm.

Minor also a Partner

In a partnership, minor cannot become co-partner though he may be admitted to the benefit of partnership. In a Joint Hindu Family firm minor is a partner.

Dissolution

The Joint Hindu Family Business can be dissolved only at the will of all the members of the family. Any single member has no right to get the business dissolved.

6. *Partnership*

The term partnership is used to mean a business structure wherein two or more Individuals, come together for undertaking a lawful business and have agreed to share the profits and losses arising from it. The management and operation of the business should be performed either by all the partners or any of them, acting for all the partners.

Characteristics of Partnership

- **Membership**: At least two persons are required to begin a partnership while the maximum number of members is limited to 100. Further, all the individuals entering into partnership must be legally competent to do so, as they have to enter into a contract to become partners. Thus, minors, insolvent and lunatic persons cannot become members, but a minor can be admitted to partnership, to share profits.
- **Unlimited liability**: The members of a partnership have unlimited liability, i.e. they are collectively and individually liable for the firm's debts and obligations. So, if in case business assets are not adequate to repay liabilities, personal assets of all or any partner can be claimed by the creditors to realize the outstanding amount.
- **Sharing of profit and loss**: The main purpose of the partnership is to share profit in the agreed ratio. However, in the absence of any agreement between partners, the business profits or losses are divided equally among all the partners.
- **Mutual Agency**: The partnership business is undertaken by all the partners or any of the partner, who acts on behalf of all the partners. So, every partner is a principal as well as an agent. Further, the acts of partners bind each other as well as the firm.
- **Voluntary Registration**: The registration of partnership is not mandatory, but it is recommended, as it offers certain benefits, **e.g.** in case of any conflict among partners, any partner can file suit against other partner or if there is any dispute between firm and outside party, then also the firm can file a case against that party.
- **Continuity**: There is a lack of continuity in partnership, like death, bankruptcy, retirement or insanity of any partner can lead the partnership to end. Although, if the remaining partners want to continue operations, they can do so by a fresh agreement.
- **Contractual Relationship**: The relation subsisting between partners is due to the contract, which may be oral, written or implied.

- **Transfer of interest**: Mutual consent of all the partners is a must for transferring the interest in the firm to any external party.

7. *Co-operative*

Co-operative banks serve an important role in the Indian Economy, especially in rural areas. They are regulated by the Reserve Bank of India. Under the banking regulation act 1949 and banking laws co-operative societies act 1965. In 1904, the co-operative credit society act was enacted to encourage co-operative movement in India. Co-operative banks are small size units organized in the co-operative sector which operate both in urban and non-urban regions. A co-operative bank is a financial entity which belongs to its members, who create the same time the owners and the customers of their bank. Co-operative banks are often created by persons belonging to the same local or professional community or sharing a common interest. The major role of co-operative banks to provide agriculture credit to the farmers for short, medium and long term.

Under the co-operative societies Act, the three-tier system for short term credit and two-tier system for term credit disbursement have been into boost in the structure of co-operatives in the state. The three-tier system consists of the Tamil Nadu state apex co-operative bank limited (State level), the district central co-operative banks (district level) and primary agricultural co-operative banks (village level). The two-tier system consists of Tamil Nadu state Apex Land Development Bank Limited (state level) and primary land development banks (village level).

8. *Limited Liability Partnership*

LLP stands for Limited Liability Partnership. It is an alternative corporate business form which offers the benefits of limited liability to the partners at low compliance costs. It also allows the partners to organize their internal structure like a traditional partnership. A limited liability partnership is a legal entity, liable for the full extent of its assets. The liability of the partners, however, is limited. Hence, LLP is a hybrid between a company and a partnership. But it should not be confused with limited liability company.

Features

- **LLP is a body corporate:** According to Section 3 of the Limited Liability Partnership Act (LLP Act), 2008, an LLP is a body corporate formed and incorporated under the Act. It is a legal entity separate from its partners.

- **Perpetual Succession:** Unlike a general partnership firm, a limited liability partnership can continue its existence even after the retirement, insanity, insolvency or even death of one or more partners. Further, it can enter into contracts and hold property in its name.
- **Separate Legal Entity:** Just like a corporation or a company, it is a separate legal entity. Further, it is completely liable for its assets. Also, the liability of the partners is limited to their contribution in the LLP. Hence, the creditors of the limited liability partnership are not the creditors of individual partners.
- **Mutual Agency:** Another difference between an LLP and a partnership firm is that independent or unauthorized actions of one partner do not make the other partners liable. All partners are agents of the LLP and the actions of one partner do not bind the others.
- **LLP Agreement:** The rights and duties of all partners are governed by an agreement between them. Also, the partners can devise the agreement as per their choice. If such an agreement is not made, then the Act governs the mutual rights and duties of all partners.
- **Artificial Legal Person:** For all legal purposes, an LLP is an artificial legal person. It is created by a legal process and has all the rights of an individual. It is invisible, intangible and immortal but not fictitious since it exists.
- **Common Seal:** If the partners decide, the LLP can have a common seal [Section 14(c)]. It is not mandatory though. However, if it decides to have a seal, then it is necessary that the seal remains under the custody of a responsible official. Further, the common seal can be affixed only in the presence of at least two designated partners of the Limited Liability Partnership.
- **Limited Liability:** According to Section 26 of the Act, every partner is an agent of the LLP for the purpose of the business of the entity. However, he is not an agent of other partners. Further, the liability of each partner is limited to his agreed contribution in the Limited Liability Partnership. It provides liability protection to its partners.
- **Minimum and Maximum Number of Partners in an LLP:** Every Limited Liability Partnership must have at least two partners and at least two individuals as designated partners. At any time, at least one designated partner should be resident in India. There is no maximum limit on the number of maximum partners in the entity.
- **Business Management and Business Structure:** The partners of the Limited Liability Partnership can manage its business. However, only the designated partners are responsible for legal compliances.

- **Business for Profit Only:** Limited Liability Partnerships cannot be formed for charitable or non-profit purposes. It is essential that the entity is formed to carry on a lawful business with a view to earning a profit.
- **Investigation:** The power to investigate the affairs of a Limited Liability Partnership resides with the Central Government. Further, they can appoint a competent authority for the same.
- **Compromise or Arrangement:** Any compromise or arrangement like a merger or amalgamation needs to be in accordance with the Act.
- **Conversion into LLP:** A private company, firm or an unlisted public company can convert into an LLP in accordance with the provisions of the Act.
- **E-Filing of Documents:** If the entity is required to file any form/application/document, then it needs to be filed in an electronic form on the website www.mca.gov.in. Further, a partner or designated partner has to authenticate the same using an electronic or digital signature.

2.12. Non-Trading Concerns

Non-trading concerns are simply non-profit making entities that exist solely for the betterment of the society by providing quality services. Unlike trading concerns that sell goods and services to earn profit, the non-trading concerns accept donations and receipts from the general public, corporate entities and government to run its operations. Some of the common examples of non-trading concerns are as follows:

- Orphanages
- Sports clubs
- Civil hospitals
- Libraries
- Charities
- Government owned educational institutions
- Civil Hospitals

Sources of Income

The main sources of income for a non-trading concern are donations, fees and government or municipal grants. The income should generally be received through a proper banking channel in order to provide an audit trail.

Accounting for Non-trading Concerns

The accounting for a non-trading concern is generally as per the principles of double entry bookkeeping system. They generally only maintain a cash book to record receipts and payments made during the year. The cash book is converted into receipt and payment account at the end of the year. The receipts and payments account is a summarized form of cash book and is considered a more useful source of information for preparing final accounts of the entity. By using information from receipt and payment account and from other sources, the entity prepares its income and expenditure account and balance sheet at the end of the period. The income and expenditure account shows a surplus or deficit for the year and balance sheet shows the assets and liabilities of the entity at the end of the year.

Management and Control

The responsibility for the management and control of a non-trading concern rests with the board of trustees who came together to make the organization in the first place.

Chances of Fraud

There is a medium to high risk of fraud in a non-trading concern as individuals within the organization may misappropriate donations or grants received and run away with the money. Therefore, the control over assets is generally very strict. Only some certain trusted individuals have access to the assets of the organization. Moreover, the operations of non-trading concerns are closely watched and regulated by the government through strict laws.

Characteristics of Non-Trading Concerns

The main characteristics of non-trading concerns are as follows:

- **Objective:** The main objective of non-trading concerns is to provide goods or services that fulfill a social need. There is neither a profit motive nor an expectation of earning net income.
- **Source of Income:** The main sources of income of non-trading concerns are fees, subscriptions, donations, Govt. and municipals grants and other similar sources.
- **Distribution of Income:** No part of excess of income over expenditure is distributed to those who contributed support through subscription or donations etc.
- **Utilization of Income:** The excess of income over expenditure is ordinarily utilized in later years to provide better goods and services to the citizens of the area.

- **Management:** The control and management of non-tracing concerns rests in the hands of trustees or governing body committee of management. Maintenance of Accounts. The accounts of these institutions are generally maintained according to the double entry bookkeeping system. At the end of the year, they make out the summary called income and expenditure summary and balance sheet. These institutions and societies do not maintain a full set of books but only cash book is maintained in which all receipts and payments are entered.

UNIT - III

CHEQUE

3.1. Definition (Cheque)

Cheque refers to a negotiable instrument that contains an unconditional order to the bank to pay a certain sum mentioned in the instrument, from the drawer's account, to the person to whom it is issued, or to the order of the specified person or the bearer.

Cheque is a negotiable instrument used to make payment in day-to-day business transaction minimizing the risk and possibility of loss. It is used by individuals, businesses, corporate and others to transact for making and receiving payment

Parties to Cheque

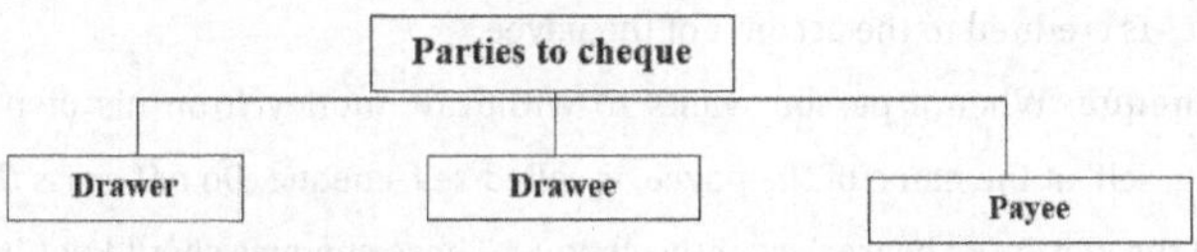

Basically, there are three parties to a cheque:

Drawer: The person who draws the cheque, i.e. signs and orders the bank to pay the sum.

Drawee: The bank on which the cheque is drawn or who is directed to pay the specified sum written on the cheque.

Payee: The beneficiary, i.e. to whom the amount is to be paid.

Apart from these three, there are two more parties to a cheque:

- **Endorser**: When a party transfers his right to take the payment to another party, he/she is called endorser.
- **Endorsee**: The party in whose favour, the right is transferred, is called endorsee. Sometimes, the drawer and payee can be the same person, when the drawer writes a self-cheque.

Types of Cheque

- **Open Cheque**: Otherwise called as uncrossed cheque, it is one on which cash is payable at the counter of the bank, or it is transferred to the bank account of the person whose name is written on the cheque. It is negotiable, i.e. it is transferable in nature.

- **Bearer Cheque**: Bearer cheque refers to the cheque which can be encashed by the person whose name is written on the cheque or anyone who presents the cheque before the bank for payment. It is negotiable in nature, which can be transferred by simply delivering it and so endorsement is not needed. No identification of the presenter or holder is required in case of a bearer cheque.
- **Order Cheque**: As the name suggests, it is the cheque which becomes payable to the person or organization whose name is specified on the cheque or to his order. To convert a bearer cheque into an order cheque, the word 'or bearer' is stricken off from the cheque. Endorsement of the cheque to the third party is done by simply signing on the cheque.
- **Crossed Cheque**: You might have observed, two transverse parallel lines at the top left corner of some cheques, which may or may not have the words – & Co., A/c payee or Non-Negotiable. Such cheques are regarded as crossed cheques. The amount on such cheques is credited to the account of the payee.
- **Self Cheque**: When a person wants to withdraw money from his own account, by writing 'self' at the name of the payee, is called self-cheque. Do not cross the cheque or cancel the words 'or bearer' from the cheque. These cheques should not be crossed, as well as the words 'or bearer' should not be stricken off from the cheque, so that any person as your representative can receive the amount on your behalf.
- **Blank Cheque**: A cheque which is only signed, but the name of the payee and date is not indicated, is called a blank cheque. Such cheques can be made account payee, and the maximum limit of withdrawal can be mentioned.
- **Stale Cheque**: A cheque bears a date and is valid up to three months of the stated date. If a cheque is presented before the bank, after the expiry of the reasonable period, i.e. three months after the date, then it is called stale cheque.
- **Post-Dated Cheque**: When a cheque is drawn containing a future date, it is called post-dated cheque. In such cases, money will not be payable by the bank before that date.
- **Ante-dated Cheque**: A cheque containing a prior date, is called an ante-dated cheque. Bank honours cheques until three months to the date mentioned.
- **Banker's Cheque**: Otherwise called a pay order, it is a non-negotiable instrument, which is issued by the bank on behalf of the customer, which is payable in the same city.
- **Cancelled Cheque**: Due to any kind of mistakes while writing the cheque, it is cancelled, and so it is called cancelled cheque.

- **Mutilated Cheque**: A cheque which is torn, damaged, crushed or washed, is called a mutilated cheque. Such cheques are honoured only when certain details are visible, after confirming with the drawer.
- **Traveler's Cheque**: A cheque issued by a bank for a fee, containing a fixed amount. These cheques are enchased or used to make payment in a foreign country, after endorsement by the signature of the holder.
- **Gift Cheque**: Cheques that are used for the purpose of gifts and prizes, usually very large in size, are called Gift Cheques. Banks charge a fee for issuing such cheques.

Essential Characteristics of a Cheque

- **It must be in writing:** A cheque must be in writing. An oral order to pay does not constitute a cheque.
- **It should be drawn on banker:** It is always drawn on a specified banker. A cheque can be drawn on a bank where the drawer has an account, saving bank, or current.
- **It contains an unconditional order to pay:** A cheque cannot be drawn so as to be payable conditionally. The drawer's order to the drawee bank must be unconditional and should not make the cheque payable dependent on a contingency. A conditional cheque shall be invalid.
- **It should be signed by the drawer and should be dated:** A cheque does not carry any validity unless signed by the original drawer. It should be dated as well.
- **The check must have an order to pay a certain sum:** The cheque should contain an order to pay a certain sum of money only. If a cheque is drawn to do something in addition to, or other than to pay money, it cannot be a cheque. **For example**, if a cheque contains '*Pay USD 500 and a TV worth USD 500 to A*' it is not a cheque.
- **It should be signed by the drawer and should be dated:** A cheque does not carry any validity unless signed by the original drawer. It should be dated as well.
- **It is payable on demand:** A cheque is always payable on demand.
- **Validity:** A cheque is normally valid for six months from the date it bears. Thereafter it is termed as stale cheque. A post-dated or antedated cheque will not be invalid. In both cases, the validity of the cheque is presumed to commence from the date mentioned on it.
- **It may be payable to the drawer himself:** Cheques may be payable to the drawer himself/herself. It may be drawn payable to bearer on demand unlike a bill or a pro-note.

- **Banker is liable only to the drawer:** The banker on whom the cheque is drawn shall be liable only to the drawer. A holder or bearer has no remedy against the banker if a cheque is dishonored.
- **It does not require acceptance and stamp:** Unlike a bill of exchange, a cheque does not require acceptance on part of the drawee. There is, however, a custom among banks to mark cheques as 'good' for the purpose of clearance. But this marking is not an acceptance. Similarly, no revenue stamp is required to be affixed on cheques.

3.2. Difference between Cheque and Bills of Exchange

Cheque

- A cheque is a type of instrument used for making payment to any individual.
- It is an absolute order which addresses the drawee to pay on behalf of the drawer to the payee.
- It is always due on demand for a fixed sum of money and signed by the drawer of the instrument.
- For payment of the cheque, an issuer and payee must have a bank account.
- The validity of cheque payment is 3 months and after the expiry of validity, a cheque will be dishonoured.

Bills of Exchange

- A bill of exchange is an unconditional negotiable instrument of payment which directs a drawee to make payment for a certain amount of money to the payee.
- A bill of exchange is approved by the drawer and affirmed by the drawee which has a predetermined date on which the payment is to be done to the payee.
- Bill of exchange is an order to pay to the payee, not a promise or request which must be signed by the drawer.
- In a bill of exchange, there is a grace period of 3 days when it becomes due.

Difference between Cheque and Bill of Exchange

Cheque	Bill of Exchange
Meaning	
The Cheque is a document which contains an order to a bank to pay fixed amount of money from the account of the client	A bill of exchange is a negotiable instrument which orders to drawee to pay a fixed amount of money to payee on demand
Existence	

A cheque exists in section 6 of the Negotiable Instruments Act, 1881.	A bill of exchange exists in section 5 of the negotiable instruments act, 1881.
Grace period	
A cheque has no grace period once it is presented for the payment.	A bill of exchange has three days of grace period.
Approved	
A Cheque does not need any approval from the parties before presented for payment.	A bill of exchange needs an approval from the drawee for the payment.
Validity	
A cheque has a validity of 3 months.	A bill of exchange has no validity for the payment.
Liability	
Parties remain liable to pay also in case notice of dishonor is not given.	In the bill of exchange, the parties who do not get notice of dishonor are free from the liability of paying.
Notice of Dishonour	
In cheque, notice of dishonor is not compulsory.	In a bill of exchange, notice of dishonor is mandatory.

3.3. Proper Drawings of Cheque

Omit the Words 'OR BEARER' and Add 'A/C Payee' at the Top Left Corner of the Cheque

Cutting the words 'Or Bearer' and writing 'A/C Payee' to the top left corner of the cheque will ensure that no one apart from the individual in whose favour this cheque is drawn can acquire the stated amount. In case you do not omit the words 'Or Bearer', it can be acknowledged as a Bearer cheque and any person possessing the cheque can claim the money.

Avoid Leaving Spaces

Always make sure that you do not leave spaces between the words PAY and the Name of the Receiver. Also, avoid leaving spaces between the name and surname. This practice is important since it doesn't offer anyone a chance to fill in alphabets before or after the name to claim the money.

Always Write 'ONLY' After Mentioning the Amount in Words in the 'RUPEES' Column with Using the Symbol '/- 'at the End

It is important to write the words 'ONLY' after you fill the amount in words. Further, after writing the numbers always put a 'slash' followed by a hyphen. Moreover, just like writing the

Name; do not maintain any space before writing the particular amount in words along with the numbers. If this tip isn't followed; the amounts can be altered by any individual, creating a difficult situation for you.

Don't Sign on the MICR Band

MICR band is the bank's related numeric at the bottom of the cheque. For everyone who is accessing the cheque mode of payment to manage transactions, it is quite crucial to know that signing in the MICR Band is considered as a WRONG practice. This is one of the prime reasons that can get your cheque defiled. Whenever you try to fill a cheque be careful to sign on the space provided right above the Name of the Account Holder or Authorized Signatory text.

Fill the Correct Date

Writing a cheque without adding the date can be a dangerous practice. This permits anyone to put any date and pull-out cash using the cheque at their will. Further, a cheque with a post- or pre-date is another issue that can lead to dishonoring of the cheque. Moreover, a wrongly written date, for example, the wrong year or a month would also lead you in a problem.

Never Ever Overwrite

When you are writing a cheque, make sure there is no sort of overwriting. It means, no scribbling or cancellation of text would be entertained by the banks. The person has to rewrite on a new cheque, if there is any overwriting mistake with the earlier cheque.

Keep Actual Records of Your Cheques

What is cheque's safety? It basically points to the careful preservation or proper maintenance of all your cheque records. One should manage a record of the cheque details comprising the cheque number, issuer name, and date for future safety reference. Do not forget to mention the payment amount with every cheque that is issued. Usually, cheque books do consist of a section for all such information at the extreme back. However, try to keep this information handy in order to avoid any kind of confusion, suspicious activity, or possible fraud.

Common Safety Measures for Writing a Cheque

- One needs to destroy all cancelled cheques until and unless they are used for any particular purpose of submission for ECS.
- Make sure you do not hand over a cheque without the presence of date, amount of cheque in numbers and words and Payee name.

- Keep your signature clear and if needed sign twice to ensure that the cheque is not bounced due to signature mismatch.
- Further, mention the credit card number, mobile number, connection number etc., on the reverse side of the cheque while you make payments towards bills for utilities.
- It is strictly prohibited to staple, disfigurer fold cheque or any sort of damage of MICR Band.

Different banks across India have stated specific guidelines regarding the proper filling of cheques. It is important to go through your bank's guidelines for acquiring proper awareness. Further, do not miss to check out conditions for cheque bounce; this would make you more alert during the cheque filling process.

Section 138 in the Negotiable Instruments Act, 1881

Section 138 in the Negotiable Instruments Act, 1881(138) Dishonour of cheque for insufficiency, etc., of funds in the account. —Where any cheque drawn by a person on an account maintained by him with a banker for payment of any amount of money to another person from out of that account for the discharge, in whole or in part, of any debt or other liability, is returned by the bank unpaid, either because of the amount of money standing to the credit of that account is insufficient to honor the cheque or that it exceeds the amount arranged to be paid from that account by an agreement made with that bank, such person shall be deemed to have committed an offence and shall, without prejudice to any other provisions of this Act, be punished with imprisonment for a term which may be extended to two years], or with fine which may extend to twice the amount of the cheque, or with both: Provided that nothing contained in this section shall apply unless—

- the cheque has been presented to the bank within a period of six months from the date on which it is drawn or within the period of its validity, whichever is earlier;
- the payee or the holder in due course of the cheque, as the case may be, makes a demand for the payment of the said amount of money by giving a notice in writing, to the drawer of the cheque, [20] [within thirty days] of the receipt of information by him from the bank regarding the return of the cheque as unpaid; and
- the drawer of such cheque fails to make the payment of the said amount of money to the payee or, as the case may be, to the holder in due course of the cheque, within fifteen days of the receipt of the said notice.

3.4. Material Alteration

Any alteration in the original state of a cheque such as date, amount, payee's name, changing the word 'order' to bearer appearing after payee's name or in endorsement is called material alteration. All material alteration must have drawer's approval with his full signature (not initials) where the alterations are made. One of the mandatory features of the CTS-2010 cheque format, prescribed by RBI, is that No changes / corrections should be carried out on the cheques (other than for date validation purposes, if required). For any change in the payee's name, courtesy amount (amount in figures) or legal amount (amount in words), etc., fresh cheque forms should be used by customers. This would help banks to identify and control fraudulent alterations.

Effects of Material Alteration

The material alteration of a cheque renders such instrument void and same cannot be enforced against any person who was a party to such instrument at the time of material alteration and did not give his/her approval to it.

The following are **not** considered as **material alteration** under N.I.Act:

- filling up of incomplete instrument (sec 20)
- Conversion of blank endorsement into a special endorsement (section 49).
- Qualifying or limiting an acceptance (section 86)
- Crossing of a cheque by holder (section 125

Case Study of Material Alteration

On merits, the learned Counsel for the appellants submitted that both the courts below misread the statement of the defendant as well as ignored the important admission of the defendant and by that, wrongly decided issue of **material alteration** against the plaintiffs. It is submitted that the defendant, in his statement, very clearly admitted that he put the girder in the shop during pendency of the suit. The learned Counsel for the appellants further vehemently submitted that in view of the fact that lot many changes were made by the defendant tenant in the suit premises then on that ground, the two courts below should have granted decree of eviction against the tenant-defendant. It is also submitted that in view of the judgment of this Court delivered in the **case** of Gurudev Singh and Ors. v. Mohammed Abdul Razak 2003(3) RLR 90 coupled with the fact that it is the defendant-tenant admitted that he who put the girder in the shop then the **case** of **material alteration** stands proved. This Court in the above **case**, upheld the concurrent finding of fact recorded by the two courts below and held that the finding of the two courts below about **material alteration** by putting girder in the basement was legally right.

Example

For instance, A drew a cheque of Rs 500 in favour of B, who **altered** the figure 500 into 5,000 without taking the consent of the maker. The instrument appeared to be drawn for Rs 5,000 on the face of it. The drawee banker paid Rs 5,000 to B on the presentment of cheque for payment.

3.5. Immaterial Alteration

An immaterial alteration is one which does not change the legal effect of the written instrument

- Thus the addition of a provision fixing the rate of interest at the legal rate where no rate had been fixed in the written contract ;
- change of the rate of interest in excess of the rate fixed by the written contract where such rate was the highest allowed by law ;
- adding "or order" to an endorsement in blank;
- adding " or bearer" to an instrument which is non-negotiable because subject to conditions ;
- and adding " payment guaranteed " over the signature of an endorser where the note waives presentment, notices and protest,
- are immaterial alterations. So where days of grace are allowed only on bills of exchange or on notes placed on the same footing, the addition of the word "fixed " to the date of maturity of a note, thereby providing against days of grace, has been held to be an immaterial alteration in case the note is never put on the footing of a bill of exchange by being discounted at a bank, though it was payable at a bank and might have been put on the footing of a bill of exchange.
- Since marginal figures are no part of a note;
- an alteration in such marginal figures,
- as changing them from $1,500 to $1,000,10 or from $000 to $650," is not a material alteration. Inserting an additional provision which has been performed before such insertion, as a provision for security which is already given,
- or an agreement to become surety on a renewal note, which has already been done,

- is immaterial. So the erasure from a building contract of a recital of receipt of the first payment, which has not in fact been made, is immaterial, since such term is not contractual and could have been contradicted by extrinsic evidence.
- In a contract between property owners and the contractor for grading a street which provided that each owner was to pay in proportion to his interest in the abutting property, an interlineations was made, " Each party hereto to pay only such parts of the total cost as his front footage bears to the total frontage improved in said street." Such interlineations were held to be immaterial.
- The addition to the correct description of realty in a mortgage the words "containing one hundred sixty acres more or less," which is the correct number, has been held immaterial.
- The addition of an internal revenue stamp has been held to be an immaterial alteration of a note payable in Massachusetts, since the Massachusetts courts have held that the provision of the Federal statutes making such instruments inadmissible in evidence if a revenue stamp is not affixed, applies only to the Federal courts and not the state courts.

Meaning

Crossing of Cheques means to draw two lines transverse parallel on left hand corner of the cheque. It directs the bank to deposit the money directly into the account and not to be pay cash at the bank counter. A crossing is an instruction to the paying banker to pay the amount of cheque to a particular banker and not over the counter. The crossing of the cheque secures the payment to a banker. It also traces the person so receiving the amount of cheque. Addition of words 'Not negotiable' or 'Account Payee only' is necessary to restrain the negotiability of the cheque. The crossing of a cheque ensures security and protection to the holder.

3.6. Types of Crossing

General Crossing

In general crossing, the cheque bears across its face an addition of two parallel transverse lines and/or the addition of words 'and Co.' or 'not negotiable' between them. In the case of general crossing on the cheque, the paying banker will pay money to any banker. For the purpose of general crossing two transverse parallel lines at the corner of the cheque are necessary. Thus, in this case, the holder of the cheque or the payee will receive the payment only through a bank account and not over the counter. The words 'and Co.' have no significance as such. But, the words 'not negotiable' are significant as they restrict the negotiability and thus, in the case of transfer, the transferee will not give a title better than that of a transferor.

Special Crossing

In special crossing, the cheque bears across its face an addition of the banker's name, with or without the words 'not negotiable'. In this case, the paying banker will pay the amount of cheque only to the banker whose name appears in the crossing or to his collecting agent. Thus, the paying banker will honor the cheque only when it is ordered through the bank mentioned in the crossing or its agent bank. However, in special crossing two parallel transverse lines are not essential but the name of the banker is most important.

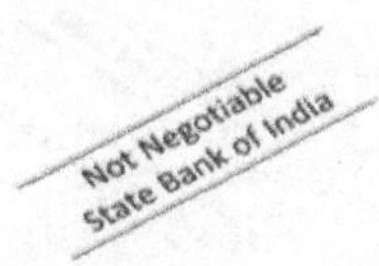

Account Payee Crossing

This type of crossing restricts the negotiability of the cheque. It directs the collecting banker that he needs to credit the amount of cheque only to the account of the payee, or the party named or his agent. Where the collecting banker credits the proceeds of a cheque bearing such crossing to any other account, customer shall be guilty of negligence. Also, customer will not be eligible for the protection to the collecting banker under section 131 of the Act. However, such crossing will have no effect on the paying banker. This is so because it is not his duty to determine that the cheque is collected for the account of the payee.

Not Negotiable Crossing

When the words not negotiable is mentioned in between the two transverse parallel lines, indicating that the cheque can be transferred but the transferee will not be able to have a better title to the cheque.

Double Crossing

Double crossing is when a bank to whom the cheque crossed specially, further submits the same to another bank, for the purpose of collection as its agent, in this situation the second crossing should indicate that it is serving as an agent of the prior banker, to whom the cheque was specially crossed. The crossing of a cheque is done to ensure the safety of payment. It is a well-known mechanism used to protect the parties to the cheque, by making sure that the payment is made to the right payee. Hence, it reduces fraud and wrong payments, as well as it protects the instrument from getting stolen or encashed by any unscrupulous individual.

Significance of Crossing

- Crossing of cheques has been discussed in Negotiable Instruments Act 1881 Section 123-131.
- Crossing provides an additional security.
- Crossing means that sum of that cheque can only recovered from a specified banker and it will be credited to the holder's account.
- The crossed cheques are not paid at the counter.
- Crossing is applicable in case of cheques only and not in case of Bill of Exchange or promissory notes.
- Crossing may be General crossing or Special crossing. General crossing (NI Act Section 123) is where a cheque bears two parallel lines with words such as a/c payee etc.
- In Special crossing (NI Act Section 124) the cheque bears the name of the banker also. Section 126 directs that such cheques shall be paid to the banker to whom it is crossed specially or to his agent for collection.

UNIT- IV

ENDORSEMENT

4.1. Definition of Endorsement

Endorsement is a term that has various definitions depending on the context of its use. For example, a signature authorizing the legal transfer of a negotiable instrument between parties is an endorsement. Endorsements can be amendments to contracts or documents such as life insurance policies or driver's licenses. A public declaration of support for a person, product, or service is also an endorsement.

Endorsements are a form of advertising that uses famous personalities or celebrities who command a high degree of recognition, trust, respect or awareness amongst the people. Such people advertise for a product lending their names or images to promote a product or service. Advertisers and clients hope such approval, or endorsement by a celebrity, will influence buyers favorably. For example, Sachin Tendulkar endorsing motorcycles and biscuits can influence young men or children who look to him as role model.

4.2. Kinds of Endorsement

According to Section 16 of the Negotiable Instrument Act, 1881, If the endorser signs his name only, the endorsement is said to be "in blank", and if he adds a direction to pay the amount mentioned in the instrument to, or to the order of, a specified person, the endorsement is said to be "in full", and the person so specified is called the "endorsee" of the instrument. There are some other kinds which are constitutional but not very popular which are given below

Endorsement in Blank or General

An endorsement is said to be blank or general when the endorser puts his signature only on the instrument and does not write the name of anyone to whom or to whose order the payment is to be made.

Endorsement in Full or Special

An endorsement is 'special' or in 'full' if the endorser, in addition to his signature also mention the name of the person to whom or to whose order the payment is to be made. There is direction added by endorse to the person specified called the endorsee, of the instrument who now becomes its payee entitled to sue for the money due on the instrument.

Conditional Endorsement

The conditional endorsement is negotiation which takes effect on the happening of a stated event, or not otherwise. Section 52 of the Negotiable Instrument Act 1881 provides - The endorser of a negotiable instrument may, by express words in the endorsement, exclude his own liability thereon, or make such liability or the right of the endorsee to receive the amount due thereon depend upon the happening of a specified event, although such event may never happen.

Where an endorser so excludes his liability and afterwards becomes the holder of the instrument all intermediates' endorsers are liable to him.

Illustrations

- The endorser of a negotiable instrument signs his name, adding the words "without recourse". Upon this endorsement, he incurs no liability.
- A is the payee and holder of a negotiable instrument. Excluding personal liability by an endorsement, "without recourse", he transfers the instrument to B, and B endorses it to C, who endorses it to A. A is not only reinstated in his former rights but has the rights of an endorsee against B and C.

Restrictive Endorsement

Restrictive endorsement seeks to put an end the principal characteristics of a Negotiable Instrument and seals its further negotiability. This may sound a little unusual, but the endorsee is very much within his rights if he so signs that its subsequent transfer is restricted. This prevents the risk of unauthorized person obtaining payment through fraud or forgery and the drawer losing his money.

Endorsement Sans Recourse

Sans Recourse which means without recourse or reference. As such a when the property in a negotiable instrument is transferred sans recourse, the endorser, negatives his liability and excludes himself from responsibility to all subsequent endorsees. It is one of the commonest forms of qualified endorsement and virtually prohibits negotiation since the endorser says in effect.

Facultative Endorsement

Facultative Endorsement is an endorsement where the endorser waives some right to which he is entitled. For example, the endorsee is liable to give notice of dishonor to the endorser and normally failure to give notice will absolve the endorser from his liability.

4.3. Paying Banker: (Meaning)

The banker who is liable to pay the value of a cheque of a customer as per the contract, when the amount is due from him to the customer is called "Paying Banker" or "Drawee Bank." The payment to be made by him has arisen due to the contractual obligation. He is also called drawee bank as the cheque is drawn on him.

The payment has to be made by the banker as per the legal obligation also. Section 31 of Negotiable Instrument Act 1881, says that "the drawee of a cheque, having sufficient funds of the drawer in his hands properly applicable to the payment of such a cheque, must pay the cheque, when duly required to do so, and in default of such payment, must compensate the drawer for any loss or damage caused by such default." According to this provision, the drawee of a cheque, *i.e.,* paying banker has a legal obligation to honour the demand of the drawer or customer. If he fails to pay the money held, he is liable for damages. Thus, paying banker has certain obligations to discharge.

Precautions to be Taken by Paying Banker while Making Payment of Cheques

The banker has to take the following precautions while honoring the cheques of his customers:

Crossed Cheque

The most important precaution that a banker should take is about crossed cheques. A banker has to verify whether the cheque is open or crossed. He should not pay cash across the counter in respect of crossed cheques. If the cheque is a crossed one, he should see whether it is general crossed or special crossed. If it is general crossing, the holder must be asked to present the cheque through some banker and should be paid to a banker. If the cheque bears a special crossing, the banker should pay only the bank whose name is mentioned in the crossing.

Open Cheque

If it is an open cheque, a banker can pay cash to the payee or the holder across the counter. If the banker pays against the instructions as indicated above, he is liable to pay the amount to the true owner for any loss sustained. Further, a banker loses statutory protection in case of forged endorsement.

Proper Form

A banker should see whether the cheque is in the proper form. That means the cheque should be in the manner prescribed under the provisions of the Negotiable Instruments Act. It should not contain any condition.

Presentment of Cheque

Presentation of the cheque should be in right format and right place. A banker can honour the cheques provided it is presented with that branch of the bank where the drawer has an account or another branch if it is multi-city cheque.

Date of the Cheque

The paying banker has to see the date of the cheque. It must be properly dated. It should not be either a post-dated cheque or a stale-cheque. If a cheque carries a future date, it becomes a post-dated cheque. If the cheque is presented on the date mentioned in the cheque, the banker need not have any objection to honour it. If the banker honours a cheque before the date mentioned in the cheque, he loses statutory protection. If the drawer dies or becomes insolvent or countermands payment before the date of the cheque, he will lose the amount. The undated cheques are usually not honored.

Words and Figures

The amount of the cheque should be expressed in words, or in words and figures, which should agree with each other. When the amount in words and figures differ, the banker should refuse payment. However, Section 18 of the Negotiable Instruments Act provides that, where there is difference between the amount in words and figures, the amount in words is the amount payable. If the banker returns the cheque, he should make a remark 'amount in words and figures differ'.

Alterations and Overwriting

The banker should see whether there is any alteration or over-writing on the cheque. If there is any alteration, it should be confirmed by the drawer by putting his full signature. The banker should not pay a cheque containing material alteration without confirmation by the drawer. The banker is expected to exercise reasonable care for the detection of such alterations. Otherwise, he has to take risk. Material alterations make a cheque void.

Proper Endorsements

Cheques must be properly endorsed. In the case of bearer cheque, endorsement is not necessary legally. In the case of an order cheque, endorsement is necessary. A bearer cheque always remains a bearer cheque. The paying banker should examine all the endorsements on the cheque before making payment

4.4. Payment in Due Course

Payment in due course means payment of a negotiable instrument at or after its date of maturity, made to its holder in good faith and without notice of any defect in his title.

Statutory Protection for Paying Banker

The paying banker should take the following protection, in order to protect himself and customer's interest, while making the payment of his customer's cheques:

Protection Regarding the Order Cheque

In case of an order cheque, Section 85(1) of the NI Act provides statutory protection to the paying banker as follows, where a cheque payable to order purports to be endorsed by or on behalf of the payee, the drawee is discharged by payment in due course.

Protection in Case of Bearer Cheques

Section 85 (2) of the Negotiable Instruments Act, 1881 states,"Whereas a cheque is originally expressed to be payable to bearer, the drawee is discharged by payment in due course to the bearer thereof, notwithstanding any endorsement whether in full or in blank appearing thereon, notwithstanding that any such endorsement purports to restrict or exclude further negotiation."

Protection in Case of Crossed Cheques

Regarding payment of crossed cheque, the paying banker gets the protection under Section 128 of the Negotiable Instruments Act, 1881: "Whereas the banker on whom a crossed cheque is drawn has paid the same in due course, the banker paying the cheque and the drawer thereof (in case such cheque has come to the hands of the payee) shall be entitled respectively to the same rights and placed in the same position if the amount of the cheque had been paid to and received by the true owner thereof."

Protection in Case of Draft

Section 85A of the NI Act states that, Drafts drawn by one branch of a bank on another payable to order where any draft, that is an order to pay money, drawn by one office of a bank upon another office of the same bank for a sum of money payable to order on demand, purports to be endorsed by or on behalf of the payee, the bank is discharged by payment in due course.

4.5. Dishonour of Cheque

A cheque is said to be dishonored when it is refused to accept or pay when presented to the bank. It is a condition in which the paying banker does not pay the amount of the cheque to the payee.

Circumstances or Reasons for Dishonour of Cheques

A paying banker must refuse payment on cheques, issued by his customers, in the following circumstances:

- **Insufficiency of funds:** When adequate funds are not available in the account of a customer, then the cheque can be dishonored. If the banker pays a countermanded cheque, he will not only be required to reverse the entry but also be held liable to pay damages for dishonoring the cheques presented subsequently which would have been honoured otherwise.
- **Notice of the Customer's Death:** The banker should not make payments on cheques presented after the death of the customer. He should return the cheque with the remark 'Drawer Deceased'.
- **Notice of the Customer's Insolvency:** A banker should refuse payment on the cheques soon after the customer is adjudicated as insolvent.
- **Receipt of the Garnishee Order:** Where Garnishee order is received attaching the whole amount, the banker should stop payment on cheques received after the receipt of such an order. But if the order is for a specific amount, leaving the specified amount, cheques should be honored if the remaining amount is sufficient to meet them.
- **Presentation of a postdated cheque:** The banker may refuse the cheque when the cheque is presented before the valid date.
- **Stale Cheques:** When the cheque is presented after a period of three months from the date it bears, the banker may refuse to make payment.
- **Material Alterations:** When there is material alteration in the cheque, the banker may refuse payment.
- **Drawer's Signature:** If the signature of the drawer on the cheque does not tally with the specimen signature, the banker may refuse to make payment.

4.6. Types of Dishonour

Dishonour of Cheque can be Divided into Two Categories i.e.

Rightful Dishonour

Dishonour of cheque by the drawee banker for any of the reasons specified above or for any other rightful reason. In this case there is no remedy available against the banker but the holder in due course has remedy both civil and criminal against the drawer.

Wrongful Dishonour

Dishonour of cheque by the banker due to negligence or carelessness by its employees. The drawer may bring an action against the bank for losses suffered by him. The payee has no action against the banker in this case.

Consequences of Wrongful Dishonour of Cheque

- Wrongful dishonour of the customer's cheque makes the Bank liable to compensate the customer on contractual obligations as well as for injury to his creditworthiness. A return of a cheque would cause injury to the drawer's reputation.
- Quantum of Damages is not limited to the actual pecuniary loss sustained by reason of such dishonour. When the customer is a trader, he is entitled to claim substantial damages even if he had suffered no actual pecuniary loss sustained by such dishonour, if he/she can show that his creditworthiness had suffered by the dishonour of the cheque.
- A non-trader is not entitled to recover substantial damages unless the damage he has suffered is alleged and proved as special damages, otherwise he would be entitled to nominal damages.
- The Plaintiff's evidence on the transaction was vague, ill-defined and indeterminate and further he/she had not proved any actual or special damages, unless special damages are claimed and proved nominal damages will be awarded.

4.7. Meaning of Forgery

Forgery is the false making or materially altering of records with intent to defraud, of any writing which if genuine, might apparently be of legal efficacy or the foundation of legal liability. Forgery is a false making of any writing instrument for the purpose of fraud or deceit, including every alteration of or addition to a true instrument. In the nutshell we can say that forgery is the fraudulent making or alteration of any record, deed writing, register, stamp, instrument etc.

According to **Section 463** of Indian Penal Code, 1860 defines forgery as "Whoever makes any false documents or any false electronic record or part of a document or electronic record, with intent to cause damage or injury, to the public or to any person, or to support any claim or title, or to cause any person to part with property or to tender into any express or implied contract, or with intent to commit fraud or that fraud may be committed, commits forgery.

Explanation 1- A man's signature of his own name may amount to forgery

Explanation 2- A draws a bill of exchange, upon a fictitious person and fraudulently accepts the bill in the name of such fictitious person with intent to negotiate it, A commits forgery.

Forgeries are committed by using computers. Some examples are: printing of counterfeit currency notes, certificates and stamp papers. Modern printers and scanners photocopiers are used to carry out such frauds.

Punishment of Forgery

Forgery has been made an offence and the punishment for the forgery has been provided under Section 465 of the Indian Penal Code, 1860 which states that whoever commits forgery shall be punished with imprisonment for a term which may extend to 2 years or fine or both.5

IPC deal with using a forged document as genuine, using as genuine, forged or counterfeit currency notes or bank notes is punishable under Section 498B of IPC and possession of forged or counterfeit currency notes or bank notes is punishable under Section 498C of IPC.

Remedial Measures

Both the prevention and detention of frauds through forgery are important for a bank. Forgery of signatures is the most continuing fraud in banking business. A banker as per legal obligation is supposed to know the signature of his customer and in case of any doubt he has to consult the specimen signatures of his customer, which has already been taken during the course of opening of account of a customer. The specimen signatures are always kept in safe custody of the bank. The bank should take reasonable care when the instrument has been presented either order or bearer, in case a bank pays forged instrument, he would be liable for the loss to the genuine customer

Protection Against Forgery

According to **Section 82(2) of the Negotiable Instruments Act, 1881,** gives protection only when the payee or endorsed signature is forged and the banker makes payment in due course. If a banker pays a cheque which carries a forged signature of his customer, it does not amount to payment in due course. It is so because every banker is expected to know the signature of his own customers. Hence, he/she cannot even think of claiming protection in the case of forged endorsement of the drawer. However, if the customer by his conduct enables the forgery of his signature, then the paying banker is relieved from his liability. Whether the customer has enabled the forgery or not depends upon the circumstance's fact of the case.

Liability of Paying Banker when Customer's Signature on Cheque is Forged

It is said that forgery of drawer's signature conveys no title and hence the paying banker has no authority to debit the customer's account. The paying banker should carefully ascertain that the cheque bears the genuine signature of the drawer after comparing the same with the specimen signature card filed with the bank. The account holder may change his signature but the changed signature should be available with the bank in a fresh specimen signature card. New specimen signature card must be obtained if the bank feels that there is some variation in the style or stroke of the signature.

If the signature on the cheque differs materially from the one field as specimen, banker must refuse payment thereon. Cheque with a forged signature of the drawer is nullity and gives no mandate to make any payment. Payment of cheque with forged signature of the drawer is deemed as payment without the authority of the customer and hence a breach of the implied contract between a banker and his customer.

Banker who pays a cheque with a forged signatures suffers the loss himself. Note that the banker bears this liability even if the signature of the drawer was so cleverly forged that it was difficult to detect it with reasonable degree of care and scrutiny.

In Canara Bank Vs Canara Sales Corporation (1987.2 supreme court cases 666) the company had a current account with the bank which was operated by the company's Managing Director. The company's Accountant in whose custody the cheque book was, forged the signature of the Managing Director on 42 cheque leaves totaling Rs.3,26,047.92 over a period of time. This was detected by another Accountant. On coming to know of the fraud the company demanded the amount from the bank. The bank refused to pay the amount. There upon the company filed a suit against the bank. The bank lost the suit but filed an appeal before the Supreme Court. The Supreme court dismissed the appeal on the following ground:

'Since the relationship between the customer and bank is that of creditor and debtor, the bank had no authority to make payment on a cheque containing a forged signature and not on a cheque from the cheque book issued to the society. The bank would be acting against the law in debiting the customer, with the amount of the forged cheque as there would be no mandate on the bank to pay. The Supreme Court pointed out that the document in the cheque form on which the customer's name as drawer was forged, was a mere nullity. The bank succeeds only when it would establish adoption or estoppels.

UNIT-V

COLLECTING BANKER

5.1. Meaning (Collecting Banker)

A collecting Banker is one who undertakes to collect various types of Instruments representing money in favour of his customer or his own behalf from the drawers of these instruments; some are negotiable instruments as provided for in the negotiable instruments act 1881 and some are quasi negotiable instruments.

A Collecting banker is one who undertakes to collect cheques, drafts, bill, pay order, traveller cheque, letter of credit, dividend, debenture interest, etc., on behalf of the customer. For undertaking this collection, the collecting banker will be charging commission.

Examples: ICICI Bank, HDFC Bank, SBI Bank etc.

Duties and Responsibilities of a Collecting Banker

The duties and responsibilities of a collecting banker are discussed below:

- Due care and carefulness in the collection of cheque.
- Serving notice of dishonour.
- Agent for collection.
- Payment of interest to the customer.
- Collection of bills of exchange.

Due Care and carefulness in the Collection of Cheques

The collecting banker is bound to show due care and carefulness in the collection of cheques presented to him. In case a cheque is entrusted with the banker for collection, he is expected to show it to the drawee banker within a reasonable time.

Serving Notice of Dishonour

When the cheque is dishonoured, the collecting banker is bound to give notice of the same to his customer within a reasonable time. It may be noted here, when a cheque is returned for confirmation of endorsement, notice must be sent to his customer.

Agent for Collection

In case a cheque is drawn on a place where the banker is not a member of the 'clearing-house', he may employ another banker who is a member of the clearing-house for the purpose of collecting the cheque. In such a case the banker becomes a substituted agent.

Payment of Interest to the Customer

In case a collecting banker has realised the cheque, he should pay the interest to the customer as per his (customer's) direction.

Collection of Bills of Exchange

There is no legal obligation for a banker to collect the bills of exchange for its customer. But, generally, bank gives such facility to its customers.

Duties and Responsibilities of a Collecting Banker

- Banker must take at most care while presenting the cheque for collection.
- Collecting banker must present the cheque within reasonable time.
- Notice to customer in case of dishonor of cheque.
- The banker has to credit the proceeds of the cheque to the account of the customer.
- Should undertake the collection of cheque only for customer and not for stranger.
- Must receive the payment as an agent of the customer.

Statutory Protection for Collecting Bankers

Section 131 of the Negotiable Instruments Act provides protection to a collecting banker who receives payment of a crossed cheque or draft on behalf of his customers. According to Section 131 of the Act "a banker who has, in good faith and without negligence, received payment for a customer of a cheque crossed generally or specially to himself shall not, in case the title to the cheque proves defective, incur any liability to the true owner of the cheque by reason only of having received such payment."

The protection provided by Section 131 is not absolute but qualified. A collecting banker can claim protection against conversion if the following conditions are fulfilled.

Good Faith and Without Negligence

Statutory protection is available to a collecting banker when he receives payment in good faith and without negligence. The phrase in "good faith" means honestly and without notice or interest of deceit or fraud and does necessarily require carefulness. Negligence means failure to exercise reasonable care. It is not for the customer or the true owner to prove negligence on the part of the banker. The burden of proving that he collected in good faith and without negligence is on the banker. The banker should have exercised reasonable care and diligence. What constitutes negligence depends upon facts of each case.

Following are a few examples which constitute negligence:

- Failure to obtain reference for a new customer at the time of opening the account.
- Collection of cheques payable to trust accounts" for crediting to personal accounts of a trustee.
- Collecting for the private accounts of partners, cheques payable to the partnership firms.
- Omission to verify the correctness of endorsements on cheques payable to order.
- Failure to pay attention to the crossing particularly the "not negotiable crossing."

Collection for a Customer

Statutory protection is available to a collecting banker if he collects on behalf of his customer only. If he collects for a stranger or noncustomer, he does not get such protection. As Jones apply puts if "duly crossed cheques are only protected in their collection, if handled for the customer". A bank cannot get protection when he collects a cheque as holder for value. In Great Western Railway vs London and Country Bank it was held that "the bank is entitled for protection as it received collection for an employee of the customer and not for the customer."

Acts as an Agent

A collecting banker must act as an agent of the customer in order to get protection. He must receive the payment as an agent of the customer and not as a holder under independent title. The banker as a holder for value is not competent to claim protection from liability in conversion. In case of forgery, the holder for value is liable to the true owner of the cheque.

Crossed Cheques

Statutory protection is available only in case of crossed cheques. It is not available in case uncrossed or open cheques because there is no need to collect them through a banker. Cheques, therefore, must be crossed prior to their presentment to the collecting banker for clearance. In other words, the crossing must have been made before it reached the hands of the banker for collection. If the cheque is crossed after it is received by the banker, protection is not available. Even drafts are covered by this protection. to conclude, it is necessary that the collecting banker should have acted without negligence if he/she wants to claim statutory protection under

Section 131 of the said Act. The statutory protection is available to the banker if he collects a cheque marked "Not Negotiable" for a customer, whose name is not used as the payee there-in, provided the requirements of the said sections are duly complied with.

5.2. Pay –in Slip

pay-in slip or **deposit slip** is a preprinted form which is the size of a standard check and typically comes in the back of the checkbook. It has the customer's name and account number, and customers write down how much money they want to deposit into a checking or savings account. They detail the exact amount of each physical check they are bringing to the bank and/or the exact amount of cash and coins they are depositing. Once the deposit is made at the bank, the customer is given a receipt to prove that the deposit has been made into the proper account. This is becoming a less common practice as many people are switching to direct (electronic) deposits.

Pay in slip screen is used to display the total cash and check payment amounts of 'Day Wise' and 'Agent Wise' for the selected operational entity. It also provides the service provider to select the payment amounts and generate or deposit pay-in-slip.

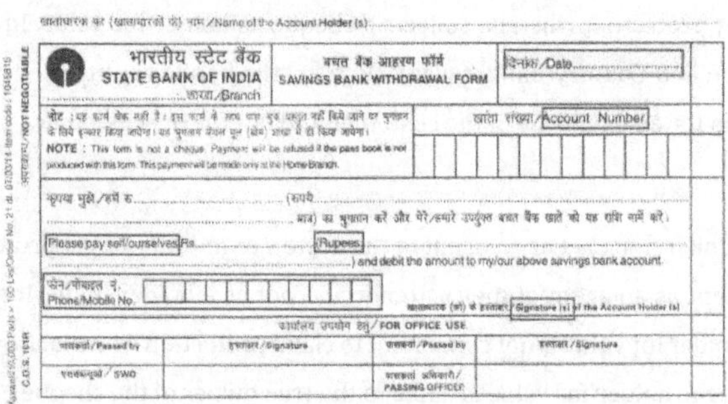
Name of the Account Holder (s)

भारतीय स्टेट बैंक
STATE BANK OF INDIA
Branch

SAVINGS BANK WITHDRAWAL FORM

Date

NOTE : This form is not a cheque. Payment will be refused if the pass book is not produced with this form. This payment will be made only at the Home Branch.

Account Number

Please pay self/ourselves Rs. (Rupees) and debit the amount to my/our above savings bank account.

Phone/Mobile No.

Signature (s) of the Account Holder (s)

FOR OFFICE USE

Passed by	Signature	Passed by	Signature
SWO		PASSING OFFICER	

NOT NEGOTIABLE

5.3. Withdrawal

A withdrawal slip is a printed piece of paper used in Bank to withdraw money in cash from account. The slip contains certain particulars such as name of customer, date, amount to be withdrawn in words and figure, signature of customer etc. However, this to be used by the account holder whose account is not with cheque facility. In case of cheque facility account, withdrawal of money can be done by cheque and no withdrawal slip is required. A withdrawal involves removing funds from a bank account, savings plan, pension, or trust. In some cases, conditions must be met to withdraw funds without penalty, and penalty for early withdrawal usually arises when a clause in an investment contract is broken.

How a Withdrawal Works?

A withdrawal can be carried out over a period of time in fixed or variable amounts or in one lump sum and as a cash withdrawal or in-kind withdrawal. A cash withdrawal requires converting the holdings of an account, plan, pension, or trust into cash, usually through a sale, while an in-kind withdrawal simply involves taking possession of assets without converting to cash.

Examples of Withdrawals

Some retirement accounts, known as IRAs, have special rules that govern the timing and amounts of withdrawals. As an example, beneficiaries must start taking the required minimum distribution (RMD), or withdrawal, from a traditional IRA by age 72. Otherwise, the person who owns the account is assessed a penalty equal to 50% of the RMD.

On the other hand, with few exceptions, an account owner must refrain from withdrawing funds until at least age 59½ or the Internal Revenue Service takes 10% of the withdrawal amount in a penalty. Financial institutions calculate the RMD based on the owner's age, the account balance, and other factors

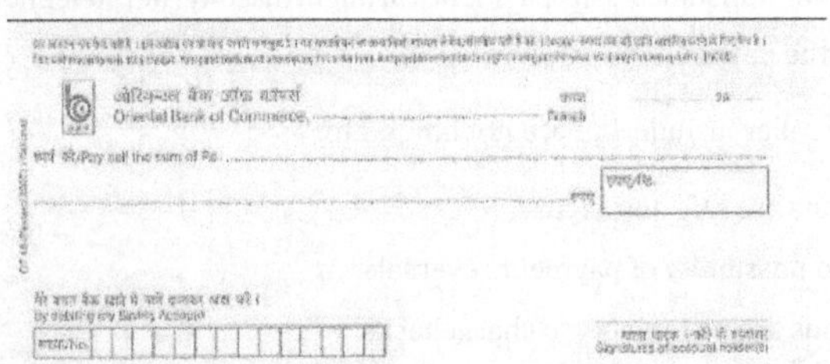

5.4. Bank Transfer

Bank transfer is the general term used to cover a wide range of credit transfers, including cash payments, giro-payments, and wire transfer to local banks. Mailing a payment form to the bank. visiting the bank and completing payment form in person. Bank transfer is the general term used to cover a wide range of credit transfers, including cash.

Customers will generally initiate a bank transfer via one of the following methods:

- online banking

- phone banking (also known as tele-banking)
- mailing a payment form to the bank
- visiting the bank and completing payment form in person

Bank transfers are characterized by the fact that they are made at the initiative of the buyer (the customer), and the payment is "pushed" to the bank account of the seller. This fact has several important consequences:

- An order is not always a payment since customers must instruct their banks to initiate the payment.
- A payment, once made, cannot be reversed by the customer. The customer can only ask the Merchant to refund the transaction.
- Although a Merchant has to rely on the customer for completing the payment, bank transfers are very safe and have no reversal risk.
- Banks worldwide are increasingly allowing their customers to initiate bank transfers online. Although this does not change the fundamentals of a bank transfer, it does allow for the transfer to clear the banks more quickly.

Benefits of Bank Transfers for the Seller

Bank transfer is commonly used by customers who do not have a credit card, or do not want to use it to complete a distance sale payment through the internet, telephone, or mail. The customer initiates the payment.

Benefits for the seller include, but are not limited to:

- Transactions are safe and secure.
- There is no possibility of payment reversals.
- Transactions are not subject to chargebacks.
- Payments are fully electronic.
- This payment method is customer-friendly.
- This payment method is increasingly popular with customers worldwide.

Drawbacks of Bank Transfers for the Seller

Drawbacks for the seller include:

- The order is not always a completed payment.
- There are potential delays in the payment completion process.

- There is the potential for payments that are not completed by the customer because the customer must contact the bank to complete the payment.

5.5. Cheque

A cheque refers to an instrument in writing which contains an unconditional order, addressed to a banker and is signed by a person who has deposited his money with the banker. This order, requires the banker to pay a certain sum of money on demand only to the bearer of cheque (person holding the cheque) or to any other person who is specifically to be paid as per instructions given.

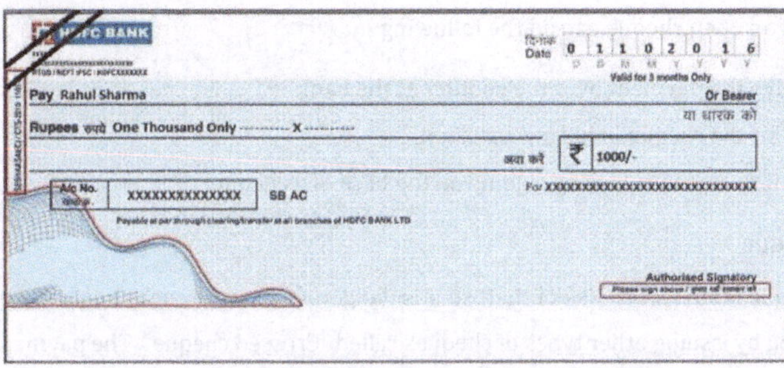

Cheques could be a good way of paying different kinds of bills. Although the usage of cheques is declining over the years due to online banking, individuals still use cheques for paying for loans, college fees, car EMIs, etc. Cheques are also a good way of keeping track of all the transactions on paper. On the other side, cheques are comparatively a slow method of payment and might take some time to be processed.

Features of a Cheque

Below given are some of the important features of a cheque

- A cheque should be in writing and properly signed by the drawer.
- A cheque contains an unconditional order.
- A cheque issued on a specified banker only.
- The amount specified is always certain and should be clearly mentioned both in figures and words. The payee of a cheque is always certain.
- A cheque is always payable on demand.
- The cheque should bear a date otherwise it is invalid and shall not be honored by the bank.

Types of Cheque

Generally speaking, cheques are of four types, they are

- Open cheque
- Crossed cheque
- Bearer cheque
- Order cheque

Open Cheque

A cheque is called „Open Cheque" when it is possible to get cash over the counter at the bank. The holder of an open cheque can do the following:

- Receive the payment over the counter at the bank
- Deposit the cheque in his own account
- Pass it to someone else by signing on the back of a cheque

Crossed Cheque

Open cheque is subject to risk of theft so it is dangerous to issue such cheques. But this risk can be avoided by issuing other types of cheques called "Crossed cheque". The payments of such cheques are not made over the counter at the bank. It is only credited to the bank account of the payee. A cheque can be crossed by drawing two transverse parallel lines across the cheque, with or without writing „Account payee" or "Not Negotiable" on it.

Bearer Cheque

A Bearer cheque is one which is payable to any person who presents it for payment at the bank counter. A bearer cheque can be transferred by mere delivery of it and it doesn"t require endorsement. It has been introduced in the Lok Sabha earlier this year on Jan 2nd, 2018. The bill seeks for amending the existing Act. The bill defines the promissory note, bill of exchange, and cheques. The bill also specifies the penalties for dishonor of cheques and various other violations related to negotiable instruments. As per a recent circular, up to INR 10,000 along with interest at the rate of 6%-9% would have to be paid by an individual for cheques being dishonored.

The Bill also inserts a provision for allowing the court to order for an interim compensation to people whose cheques have bounced due to a dishonoring party (individuals/entities at fault). Such interim compensation won't exceed 20 percent of the total cheque value.

Difference between the Cheque and Promissory Notes

S.No	Cheque	Promissory Note
1	**Meaning of Cheque:** A cheque is an order to a bank to pay a stated sum from drawer's account, written on a specially printed form.	**Meaning of Promissory Note:** A promissory note is an unconditional promise in writing made by one person to another, signed by the maker, engaging to pay on demand or at a fixed or determinable future time, a sum certain in money to the order of a specified person, or to bearer.
2	**Definition** According to Section 6 of Negotiable Instrument Act 1881, a cheque is a bill of exchange drawn on a specified banker and not expressed to be payable otherwise than on demand.	**Definition** According to Section 4 of the Negotiable Instrument Act 1881 "Promissory Note" is an Instrument in writing (not being a bank - note or a currency-note) containing an unconditional undertaking signed by the maker, to pay a certain sum of money only to, or to the order of, a certain person, or to the bearer of the Instrument.
3	There are three parties namely 1) Drawer 2) Drawee and 3) Payee	In Promissory Note, there are two parties namely 1) maker and 2) Payee
4	It can be drawn only by the account holder of a bank.	A promissory note can be made by any person.
5	In a cheque, an order for payment is given to the bank	In a promissory note, there is a promise to pay
6	A cheque is payable always on demand.	It may be payable on demand or after a specified time
7	**Grace time:** Three days of grace are not given in a Cheque	**Grace time:** Three days of grace are given in promissory notes payable after a specified time.
8	The drawer and payee may be the same person.	The maker and the payee/drawer may not be the same person.
9	No stamps required to be affixed	In a promissory note, stamps are required to be Affixed.
10	Cheque can be crossed	Crossing of the promissory note is not required.

5.6. Bill of Exchange

Meaning

Bills of exchange refer to a legally binding, written document which instructs a party to pay a predetermined sum of money to the second(another) party. Some of the bills might state that money is due on a specified date in the future, or they might state that the payment is due on demand.

A bill of exchange is used in transactions pertaining to goods as well as services. It is signed by a party who owes money (called the payer) and given to a party entitled to receive money (called the payee or seller), and thus, this could be used for fulfilling the contract for payment.

However, a seller could also endorse a bill of exchange and give it to someone else, thus passing such payment to some other party. It is to be noted that when the bill of exchange is issued by the financial institutions, its usually referred to as a bank draft. And if it is issued by an individual, it is usually referred to as a trade draft. A bill of exchange primarily acts as a promissory note in the international trade; the exporter or seller, in the transaction addresses a bill of exchange to an importer or buyer. A third party, usually the banks, is a party to several bills of exchange acting as a guarantee for these payments. It helps in reducing any risk which is part and parcel of any transaction.

Specimen

Bangalore
1st June, 2018

₹4,00,000

Two months after date, pay to me or my order, the sum of
Rupees Four lakh only, for value received

STAMP

Accepted
(Signed)
Raj Kiran
14, Bangalore

(Signed)
Kunal Singh
Lal Bagh, Bangalore

Features of Bills of Exchange

- It is an instrument in writing.
- It contains an unconditional order to pay. It means that no conditions can be attached for making the payment.
- It mainly involves three parties: Drawer, Drawee and Payee.
- In most of the cases, the Drawer and Payee are the same person as the Drawer draws the bill in his/her own favor. However, it must be remembered that the Drawer and Drawee cannot be same person (Its very stupid of me to mention it but I have noticed that it helps in better understanding).
- The Parties to bills of exchange must be certain.
- The Drawer (a.k.a the Maker) must sign the bill.
- The amount of money to be paid must be certain.

Parties to Bill of Exchange

- **Drawer:** The person who makes the bill, or who gives the order to pay a certain sum of money, is the drawer of the instrument.

- **Drawee:** The person who accepts the bill of exchange, or who is directed to pay a certain sum, is called drawee.
- **Payee:** The person receiving payment is called the payee, who can be a designated person or the drawer himself.

Now, apart from the parties mentioned above, there are some other parties to a bill of exchange, described as under:

- **Drawee, in case of need:** If in any bill of exchange, a person"s name is mentioned in addition to the original drawee, who can be resorted for payment. Then, that person will be called as drawee.
- **Holder:** The holder of the bill of exchange, is the person who possesses the bill and who has the right to recover the amount from the parties.
- **Acceptor**: The person who accepts the bill is called acceptor. Usually, a debtor or drawee is the acceptor. However, it can be accepted by some other person also, on behalf of the debtor/drawee.
- **Endorser:** If the holder of the bill, endorses it to another person, then the person will be called as the endorser.
- **Endorsee**: The person to whom the bill of exchange is endorsed, is called as an endorsee.

5.7. Bill Discounting

Bill Discounting is a discount/fee which a bank takes from a seller to release funds before the credit period ends. This bill is then presented to seller's customer and full amount is collected. Bill Discounting is mostly applicable in scenarios when a buyer buys goods from the seller and the payment is to be made through letter of credit. It means that the bank will charge the interest amount for the credit period as an advance from the buyer's account. After that, the bill amount is paid as per the end of the time span with respect to the agreed upon document between the buyer and seller. Bill Discounting is a major trade activity. It helps the seller's get funds earlier on a small fees or discount. It also helps the bank earn some revenue. The borrower or (seller's) customer can pay money on the due date of the credit period.

5.8. Promissory Notes

A promissory note refers to a written promise to its holder by an entity or an individual to pay a certain sum of money by a pre - decided date. In other words, Promissory notes show the amount which someone owes to you or you owe to someone together with the interest rate and also the date of payment. **For example**, A purchases from B INR 10,000 worth of goods. In case A is not able to pay for the purchases in cash or doesn't want to do so, he could give B a promissory note. It is A"s promise to pay B either on a specified date or on demand. In another possibility, A might have a promissory note which is issued by C. He could endorse this note and give it to B and clear of his dues this way. However, the seller isn't bound to accept the promissory note. The reputation of a buyer is of great importance to a seller in deciding whether to accept the promissory note or not.

Promissory Note Template

Promissory Note

Amount: ______________________ **Date:** ______________

Place: ______________________

I Mr. ABC, make commitment to pay XYZ Company, the Sum of $ ________________.
Repayment is to be made in the form of 200 equal payments at the interest rate of 7.2% of $ __________ payable on the 1oth of each month, beginning 10/01/2011 until the total amount of debt is paid.

IN WITNESS WHEREOF, I set my hand under seal this ____ [the day] of ____________ [month], 20___ and I acknowledge receipt of a completed copy of this instrument.

____

Sign: *[Signature of borrower]*

Notary Public - SEAL

My Commission Expire ______/______/______

____

Name & Address: *[Party name]*

Characteristics of Promissory Note

- It is a written document.
- There must be a clear and unconditional promise to pay a certain sum to a specified person or on demand.
- It must be drawn and duly signed by the maker.
- It must be properly stamped.
- It specifies the name of the maker and payee.
- The amount to be paid must be certain, given in both figures and words.
- Payment is to be made in the countrys 'legal currency.
- A promissory note may consist of various terms and conditions related to indebtedness like the principal amount, date of maturity, the rate of interest, terms of repayment, issue date, name and signature of the drawer, name of the drawee and so forth. A promissory note needs no acceptance.

Types of Promissory Notes

Depending upon the kind of promissory loan, notes are of different types. Few are mentioned below.

- **Personal Promissory Notes:** This is a particular loan taken from family or friends. Though people avoid legal writings when seeking a loan from close contact, the promissory note shows belief and trust in the interest of the borrower.
- **Commercial:** Here, the note is made when dealing with commercial lenders such as banks. Most of the commercial promissory agreement is similar to personal notes.
- **Real Estate**: This is similar to commercial notes in terms of nonpayment consequences. If the borrower becomes a defaulter, then the party has the right to keep the property until the debt is cleared. It is a little risky as all the essential details become public, which can hinder the borrower's credit history in the future.
- **Investments:** The promissory note is occasionally used to raise funds for the business. It is used as a security purpose and managed by securities laws. It includes terms and conditions related to returns of investment.

All promissory notes constitute three primary parties. These include the drawee, drawer and payee.

- **Drawer**: A drawer is a borrower or debtor who promises to pay the debt to the moneylender.
- **Drawee**: She/He is an individual; in whose favor the note is prepared. She/He is the creditor and provides goods or services on credit or lends capital.
- **Payee**: A payee is someone to whom the payment is made.

Most of the times, the payee and drawee are the same people to whom the cash is paid. The party who has loaned the money keeps the promissory note, and when the due is cleared, the payee or drawee cancels the note and gives it to the drawer/payee.

Features of Promissory Note

- **Printed/Written Agreement:** A promissory should be in writing, and an oral promise to pay money is not accepted.
- **Pay Defined Amount:** It is a promise to pay the money on a particular time or when demanded. The mentioned amount can neither be added or subtracted.
- **Signed Documents:** The document is duly signed and drawn by the drawer and stamped.

- **Unconditional Promise:** The promise to pay a certain amount of money must be absolute in all cases. In such notes, a conditional guarantee is not accepted.
- **Legal Composition:** All the payment should be made in the nation's legal currency.
- **Detailed Information:** The note has all the required information including the name of the drawer and payee, date of maturity, terms of repayment, issue date, name of the drawee, name, and signature of the drawer, principal amount, and the rate of interest, etc.

5.9. Fixed Deposit Receipt

Fixed Deposits are considered the most common and risk-free savings and investment options. These options are designed to provide the depositor with guaranteed returns in the form of interest on the amount invested. The rates of interest provided on the fixed deposits are higher than what is offered on savings accounts and less than those on equities and mutual funds.

The maturity value offered on fixed deposits is generally based on the date of maturity selected by the depositor. One can procure a fixed deposit scheme by visiting the bank branch or online if the bank offers the facility through its e-portal. Once the individual completes all the formalities, they will get the Fixed Deposit Receipt (FDR) as an acknowledgement of the investment. This receipt must be kept safely since it contains important details about the investment.

What is a Fixed Deposit Receipt?

A Fixed Deposit Receipt is proof that the depositor has kept a certain amount for a specified time period at the prevailing fixed rate of interest in the bank. This receipt or document contains every single detail of the scheme. The contents of the Fixed Deposit Receipt have been mentioned below:

- Name of the depositor
- Age of the depositor
- Account details of the depositor
- Deposited amount
- Applicable rate of interest on the deposit
- Maturity date
- Interest that the depositor will get on maturity

- Deposit and scheme related instructions

This receipt acts as a proof of ownership for the individual who has opted for the scheme. Since the FDR is so important, the depositor must keep it safely and securely.

Factors to Check in the Fixed Deposit Receipt

Bank Term deposits or Fixed Deposits have become a popular investment option for people. Here are some crucial factors one needs to check in their Fixed Deposit Receipt:

Applicable Rate of Interest and Deposit Term

These are the basic things to look for in an FD receipt and it is always better to double check the details i.e. the applicable rate of interest and the maturity term of the scheme. This becomes even more important when the depositor is renewing their old fixed deposit scheme. It is because the rate of interest is subject to change from time-to-time without any prior notice. Also, sometimes the bank discontinues certain plans. If someone has renewed their fixed deposit, it is essential to cross-check the details to avoid any confusion later.

Maturity and Auto-Renewal Dates

The maturity date of the scheme is always mentioned on the deposit receipt. For specific planning or need such as gifting a sum to your daughter on her wedding or birthday or even for her higher education, it is extremely important to double check the maturity date to avoid any inconvenience later. Moreover, if the depositor has opted for the auto-renewal facility, do not forget to check the time of auto-renewal on the Fixed Deposit Receipt date.

Penalties and Charges

Some banks charge a certain amount as a penalty if the deposit is withdrawn by the depositor before the maturity of the FD or a specified time period. If there is any sort of penalty on the same, it should be on the receipt. The charges for premature withdrawal may differ from one bank or provider to another.

Nomination Details

Not all fixed deposit schemes offer this facility. FD Receipt also acknowledges if the depositor has made a nomination. To register the nomination, the applicant has to fill out a simple form. In case of an unforeseen event like the death of the depositor, the nominee will get the benefits from the FD.

5.10. Safe Custody Receipt

Safe Custody

Safe custody is the safe Keeping of important documents and valuables. Items commonly requested by customers to be held in safe custody by the bank include property deeds, a will as well as other valuables and documents. Customer require access to a safety deposit box to get the will, customers will need at least one of the proofs of death requirements (a Medical Certificate, Death certificate or a probate bond).

Safe Deposit Lockers

The Bank's Safe Deposit Locker service is available to our customers for storing the valuables for a nominal annual rent (payable in advance), which depends upon the size of the locker and the centre at which the branch is located.

5.11. Travelers Cheque (Meaning)

A traveler's cheque is a medium of exchange that can be used in place of hard currency. They can be denominated in one of a number of major world currencies and are preprinted, fixed-amount cheques designed to allow the person signing it to make an unconditional payment to someone else as a result of having paid the issuer for that privilege.

Importance

They were generally used by people on vacation in foreign countries instead of cash, as many businesses used to accept traveler's cheques as currency. The incentive for merchants and other parties to accept them lay in the fact that as long as the original signature (which the buyer is supposed to place on the cheque in ink as soon as they receive the cheque) and the signature made at the time the cheque is used are the same, the cheques issuer will unconditionally guarantee payment of the face amount even if the cheque was fraudulently issued, stolen, or lost.

This means that a traveler's cheque can never 'bounce' unless the issuer goes bankrupt and out of business. If a traveler's cheque were lost or stolen, it can be replaced by the issuing financial institution. The financial institutions issuing traveler's cheques earn income in a number of ways. Firstly, they would charge a fee on sale of such cheques. In addition, they can earn interest for the period that the cheques are uncashed, while not paying any interest to the cheque holder, making them effectively interest-free loans. Also, the foreign exchange rate commonly used on traveler's cheques (generally based on rates applicable at the time of purchase) is less favorable compared to other forms of obtaining foreign currency, especially those on credit card transactions (which use a rate applicable at the statement date). On the other hand, the set-up cost and the cost of issuing and processing traveler's cheques is much higher than for credit card transactions.

The cheque issuer carries the exchange rate risk, and would normally pay a fee to hedge against the risk. Their use has been in decline since the 1990s, when a variety of more convenient alternatives, such as credit cards, debit. Their use has been in decline since the 1990s, when a variety of more convenient alternatives, such as credit cards, Debit cards, pre-paid currency cards and automated teller machines, became more widely available and were easier for travelers to use. Traveler's cheques are no longer widely accepted and cannot easily be cashed, even at the banks that issued them. The alternatives to traveler's cheques were generally cheaper and more flexible. Travel money cards offer similar features to traveler's cheques, including pre purchase of foreign currency at rates applicable at date of purchase, but offer greater ease and flexibility, such as use like a regular credit card, no need to get change in a local currency, besides other features.

There are four parties involved in the Travelers cheque transaction:

Issuer or Obligor, an organization that produces the traveler's cheque

Agent, the bank or any other party that sells the cheque

Purchaser, the person who buys it

Payee or Merchant, a person to whom the cheque is handed over in exchange for goods and services.

The Travelers cheque can be replaced by the issuer, in case it is lost or stolen. This requires the purchaser of the cheque to maintain a copy of cheque receipt or its number in a safe custody so that it can be produced to the issuer to get the cheque replaced. The traveler's cheques are available in varied currencies such as US Dollars, Great Britain Pounds (GBP), Japanese Yen (JY), Australian Dollars (AUD) and Canadian Dollars (CAD).

5.12. Meaning of Credit Card

A credit card is a card which allows people to buy items without cash. Each card has a unique number. Payment using a credit card is one of the most common methods of electronic payment. Credit cards are usually small plastic cards with a unique number attached to an account. Credit card is a card issued by a financial institution authorizing the holder to buy goods or services on credit. Credit cards usually charge high interests and are used for short-term financing. Interests usually start one month after a purchase is made and bank sets credit limits according to the client's credit rating.

Types of Credit Card

Standard "Plain-Vanilla" Credit Cards

Standard credit cards are referred to as "plain-vanilla" credit cards because they offer no frills or rewards. They're also relatively easy to understand. Customer might choose this type of credit card if they want a card that isn't complicated and they're not interested in earning rewards. The standard credit card allows customer to have a revolving balance up to a certain credit limit. Credit is used up when you make a purchase and then more credit is made available once customer made a payment. A finance charge is applied to outstanding balances at the end of each month. Credit cards have a minimum payment that must be paid by a certain due date to avoid late-payment penalties.

Balance Transfer Credit Cards

While many credit cards come with the ability to transfer balances, a balance transfer credit card is one that offers a low introductory rate on balance transfers for a certain period of time. If customer want to save money on a high-interest rate balance on an existing card, a balance transfer is a good way to go. Balance transfer interest rates vary - some are as low as 0 percent, but these usually have qualifiers such as a minimum of two transactions a month. The lower the promotional rate (and longer the promotional period) the more attractive the card is. However, customer often need good credit to qualify.

Rewards Credit Cards

There are three basic types o f rewards cards: cash back, points, and travel. Some people prefer the flexibility of cash back rewards, while others like points that can be redeemed for cash or other merchandise. Travel rewards cards remain a favorite among frequent travelers because of the ability to earn free flights, hotel stays, and other travel perks.

Student Credit Cards

Student credit cards are those specifically designed for college students with the understanding that these young adults often have little or no credit history. A first-time credit card applicant would generally have an easier time getting approved for a student credit card than another type of credit card. Student credit cards may come with additional perks like rewards or a low-interest rate on balance transfers, but these aren't the most important features for students looking for their first credit card. Students generally have to be enrolled at an accredited four-year university to be approved for a student credit card.

Charge Cards

Charge cards do not have a preset spending limit and balances must be paid in full at the end of each month. Charge cards typically do not have a finance charge or minimum payment because the balance needs to be paid in full. Late payments are subject to a fee, charge restrictions, or card cancellation depending on your card agreement.

Secured Credit Cards

Secured credit cards are an option for people who don't have a credit history or who have damaged their credit status. Secured cards require a security deposit to be placed on the card. The credit limit on a secured credit card is typically equal to the amount of the deposit made on the card, but it could be more in some cases - such as a major default such as defaulting on a mortgage payment. It's worth noting that customers still expected to make monthly payments on customers secured credit card balance.

Subprime Credit Cards

Subprime credit cards are one of the worst credit card products. These credit cards are geared toward applicants who have a bad credit history and these cards typically have high interest rates and fees. While approval is often quick, even for those with bad credit, the terms are often confusing. The Federal government has made rules regarding the amount of fees subprime credit card issuers can charge, but the card issuers often look for loopholes and ways to skirt these rules. Despite the unattractiveness of subprime credit cards, some consumers continue to apply for the cards because they cannot get credit elsewhere. This is a situation where you have to proceed at your own risk.

Prepaid Cards

Prepaid cards require the cardholder to load money onto the card before the card can be used. Purchases are withdrawn from the card's balance. The spending limit does not renew until more money is loaded onto the card.

Prepaid cards do not have finance charges or minimum payments because the balance is withdrawn from the deposit you've made. These cards are not actually credit cards, and they don't directly help you rebuild your credit score. Prepaid cards are similar to debit cards, but are not tied to a checking account. A lot of people use them as a way to stay within budget.

Limited Purpose Cards

Limited purpose credit cards can only be used at specific locations. Limited purpose cards are used like credit cards with a minimum payment and finance charge. Store credit cards and gas credit cards are examples of limited purpose credit cards.

Business Credit Cards

Business credit cards are designed specifically for business use. They provide business owners with an easy method of keeping business and personal transactions separate. There are standard business credit and charge cards available.

Even for a business credit card, your personal credit history is considered because the credit card issuer still needs to hold an individual accountable for the credit card balance.

5.13. Letter of Credit (Meaning)

A letter of credit is a document that guarantees the buyer's payment to the sellers. It is Issued by a bank and ensures the timely and full payment to the seller. If the buyer is unable to make such a payment, the bank covers the full or the remaining amount on behalf of the buyer. A letter of credit is issued against a pledge of securities or cash. Banks typically collect a fee, ie, a percentage of the size/amount of the letter of credit.

Definition

A letter of credit, or "credit letter" is a letter from a bank guaranteeing that a buyer's payment to a seller will be received on time and for the correct amount. In the event that the buyer is unable to make a payment on the purchase, the bank will be required to cover the full or remaining amount of the purchase. It may be offered as a facility.

Due to the nature of international dealings, including factors such as distance, differing laws in each country, and difficulty in knowing each party personally, the use of letters of credit has become a very important aspect of international trade.

How a Letter of Credit Works?

Because a letter of credit is typically a negotiable instrument, the issuing bank pays the beneficiary or any bank nominated by the beneficiary. If a letter of credit is transferable, the beneficiary may assign another entity, such as a corporate parent or a third party, the right to draw. Banks also collect a fee for service, typically a percentage of the size of the letter of credit. The International Chamber of Commerce Uniform Customs and Practice for Documentary Credits oversees letters of credit used in international transactions. There are several types of letters of credit available.

Types of Letter of Credit

Commercial Letter of Credit

This is a standard letter of credit that's commonly used in international trade, and may also be referred to as a documentary credit or an import/export letter of credit. A bank acts as a neutral third party to release funds when all the conditions of the agreement have been met.

Standby Letter of Credit

This type of letter of credit is different: It provides payment if something *fails* to happen. Instead of facilitating a transaction, a standby letter of credit provides compensation when something goes wrong. Standby letters of credit are very similar to commercial letters of credit, but they are only payable when the payee (or "beneficiary") proves that they didn't get what was promised. Standby letters of credit are like insurance that you'll get paid, and they can be used to ensure that services will be performed satisfactorily.

Confirmed (And Unconfirmed) Letters of Credit

When a letter of credit is confirmed, another bank (presumably one that the beneficiary trusts) guarantees that payment will be made. Exporters might not trust a bank that issues a letter of credit on behalf of a buyer (because the exporter is not familiar with that bank, for example, and is not sure if payment will ever arrive), so they might require that a bank in their home country confirm the letter. If the issuing bank fails to pay—and the exporter can meet all of the requirements of the letter of credit—the confirming bank will have to pay the exporter (and try to collect from the issuing bank later).

Back-to-Back Letters of Credit

A back-to-back letter of credit allows intermediaries to connect buyers and sellers. Two letters of credit are used so that each party gets paid individually: An intermediary gets paid by the buyer, and a supplier gets paid by the intermediary. The final buyer and the intermediary use a "master" letter of credit, and the intermediary and supplier use a letter of credit based on the master letter.

Revolving Letters of Credit

A revolving letter of credit can be used for multiple payments. If a buyer and seller expect to do business continually, they may prefer not to obtain a new letter of credit for every transaction (or for every step in a series of transactions). This type of letter of credit allows businesses to use a single letter of credit for numerous transactions until the letter expires (typically up to one year).

Sight Letter of Credit

Payment under a sight letter of credit occurs as soon as the beneficiary submits acceptable documents to the appropriate bank. The bank has a few days to review the documents and ensure that they meet the requirements in the letter of credit. If the documents are compliant, payment is made immediately.

Deferred Payment Letter of Credit

With this type of letter of credit, payment does *not* happen immediately after the documents are accepted. Some agreed-to period of time passes before the seller is paid. A deferred payment letter of credit is naturally a better deal for buyers than for sellers. These are also known as term or usance letters of credit.

Red Clause Letter of Credit

With a red clause, the beneficiary has access to cash up front. The buyer allows for an unsecured loan to be issued as part of the letter of credit, which is essentially an advance on the rest of the payment. The seller or beneficiary can then use the money to buy, manufacture, or ship goods to the buyer.

Irrevocable Letter of Credit

An irrevocable letter of credit cannot be changed without authorization from all parties involved. Almost all letters of credit now are irrevocable, because revocable letters of credit simply do not provide the security that most beneficiaries want.

REFERENCES

[1] Dr.P. Narayanasamy, Assistant professor, Department of Economics, APSA College Tirupathur, Banking Law & Practice, Directorate of Distance Education, Alagappa University, Karaikudi.

[2] Neha Gupta (2019), International Journal of Law Management & Humanities, Forgery: An Offence under Banking Sector, Volume 2, Issue 2, ISSN: 2581-5369.

[3] The Institute of Company secretaries of India (2014), Banking law & Practice.

[4] Shivam Goel (2018), The Negotiable Instruments Act, 1881: Critical Analysis, SSRN Electronic journal.

[5] A.A. shelyuk (2013), Research of Components of the system of bank deposit Management, Journal of Governance and Regulation, Vol.2.Issue.1, 2013.

[6] C.J Nagel at.al (2015), The Banker- customer Relationship: Negligence in the payment and collection of cheques, https://www.researchgate.net/publication/228126514.

[7] https://rbidocs.rbi.org.in/rdocs/Bulletin/PDFs/2BANKDEPOSITES98924A19273E45 6993982E67B77B36CA.PDF

[8] Prof. Suplab Podder, Paying Banker and collecting Banker, http://skpodder.co.in/.

[9] http://bankessentials.blogspot.com/2012/10/chapter-5-collecting-and-paying-banker.html